971·06
NF1

D0752629

S40
. N40
1972
c. 2

The Politics of Chaos

ATLANTIC BAPTIST COLLEGE
MONCTON, N. B.

The Politics of Chaos

CANADA IN THE THIRTIES

H. Blair Neatby

MACMILLAN OF CANADA/TORONTO

©H. Blair Neatby, 1972

All rights reserved — no part of this book
may be reproduced in any form without
permission in writing from the publisher,
except by a reviewer who wishes to quote
brief passages in connection with a review
written for inclusion in a magazine or
newspaper.

ISBN 7705 - 0853 - 7 — cloth
         7705 - 0867 - 7 — paper
Library of Congress Catalogue Card No.
70 - 187791

PHOTO CREDITS

Chapters 2, 4, 5, 6, 7 and 9—The Public
Archives of Canada
Chapters 1 and 11—The Toronto Public
Library, Baldwin Room
Chapter 3—The Toronto Star Syndicate
Chapter 10—The *Globe and Mail*

Design by Peter Maher

Printed in Canada by The Bryant Press for
The Macmillan Company of Canada Limited
70 Bond Street, Toronto

Contents

ATLANTIC BAPTIST COLLEGE
MONCTON, N. B.

The Politics of Chaos

Introduction

The fascination for the 1930s is relatively recent. For those who lived through the depression the first reaction was relief that it was behind them. Only later could they remember with nostalgia the personal bonds forged by common hardships and economic disaster. For the younger generation, the 1930s is now part of history, a remote prewar decade, tinged with the romance of a period when life seems to have been simpler and less confusing. But this contemporary vogue for the 1930s is also linked to the concern for Canadian identity. In many ways the decade marks the beginning of modern Canada. The Canadians of that era were grappling almost for the first time with many of the problems which are still with us. A study of the 1930s is an introduction to the Canada of today.

This book describes the variety of responses to the

problems of the era. It is a study of politics because politics dominated all discussions. It is biographical in its approach, not merely because Canadian politicians of the 1930s were colourful characters but also because they illustrate the diversity of responses during the decade. The introductory chapters sketch the social and political context in which these men operated. Many more individuals could have been included. There are no Maritime politicians because the sources for these men are inadequate; others had to be ignored because of space limitations. The selection is no more than an introduction to the politics of the decade.

The book began as a series of television lectures. I am indebted to Miss Nancy Fraser of CJOH-TV who produced the programs for the University of the Air. I am grateful to her for editing the scripts and also for her wide-ranging research for the graphics, some of which have been used as illustrations for this volume. The lectures have been revised and reorganized but the style is still popular rather than pedantic. I hope it is both readable and academically respectable.

1
The Question of Identity

What did it mean to be a Canadian in the 1930s? There was no simple answer to this question; Canadians came in all sorts and sizes. A Canadian might be French- or English-speaking; he might be a farmer, a factory worker or a lawyer; he might call himself a Maritimer or a British Columbian and believe that this established his identity. <u>The cultural, social and regional differences in Canada had always been so marked that it had never been easy to say what Canadians had in common</u>. The 1930s were no exception.

The decade of the 1930s was distinctive, however, because it was one of those periods when Canadians became obsessed with the problem of their identity. <u>The relationship with Great Britain was clearly changing. The Statute of Westminster of 1931 formally de-</u>

clared that Canada was no longer a British colony but was less clear about what it had become. It was autonomous; everybody could agree on that. But what did autonomy mean? Clearly it did not mean that Canada was a nation like other nations. There had been no Declaration of Independence to mark its birth and no definition of autonomy to describe its status. It was neither flesh nor fowl; it was not a colony and yet it was not an independent country. Nobody could be sure what it was.

Canadian status was not an academic question. The 1930s was an era of intense national rivalries, a decade always on the verge of war. If Great Britain went to war what would Canada do? As a member of the British Commonwealth of Nations would she be automatically involved in the war? Or did autonomy mean that Canada could be neutral? For Canadians the definition of Canadian identity could mean the difference between war or peace.

Canadians argued about their status in the 1930s but they did not reach any clear decision. Some could not imagine a Canada that was not an integral part of the Commonwealth. For them to be neutral when Britain was at war would have been tantamount to treason. Others believed that autonomy was an intermediate stage between colony and nation. They saw complete independence as the eventual goal and neutrality as natural if Canadian security was not threatened. With such contradictory ideas about Canadian identity no agreement was possible. The Canadian government did not try to force the issue. Mackenzie King was convinced that any decision would alienate one of the groups and he pleaded with Canadians to wait.

When war came in 1939, Canada did stand at Britain's side and the vast majority of Canadians approved the decision. They did so, however, for a variety of reasons. For some it was enough that Britain was at war; for others it was Canada's war because democracy was in danger. The debates of the 1930s, however, had had some effect. The discussion had moved Canada further along the road to independence; a national identity separate from Great Britain was taking shape.

The problem of Canadian identity went much deeper than defining relations with the Commonwealth. If Canada was an emerging nation what kind of a nation would it be? Were there national characteristics which distinguished Canadians from citizens of other countries? For all the diversity within Canada were there some qualities which all its citizens had in common?

The 1930s was a period when Canadians began to take such questions seriously. Men argued about whether there was a distinctively Canadian culture and, for those who insisted that there was, there was still the problem of defining it. Now that the political ties with Great Britain were weakening, it was easier to identify Canada as a North American country. But were Canadians just like other North Americans, no different from the citizens of the United States, or were they North Americans with a difference? Was the way of life really the same on both sides of the international boundary?

Superficially it was not easy to distinguish Canadians from Americans. The mass culture of North America showed no respect for political boundaries. Indeed, in the province of Quebec, even language was not an impenetrable barrier. A sensitive visitor interested in popular styles and popular entertainment would have noted some regional differences and a time-lag by comparison with New York or Hollywood, but that would be all. It would have been easy to conclude that Canada was part of a mass-produced and homogenized North American society.

Even the mass culture, however, underwent some intriguing shifts during the decade. Women's styles, for example, were quite unlike the styles of the 1920s. The clothes of the earlier decade symbolized emancipation, a freedom from restraint. Skirts had been short, materials had become lighter, hair was bobbed, chests were flat, waists were ignored; all of this had been consistent with the feeling that women should be sophisticated, freed from the burdens of motherhood. This was the time when daring ladies smoked and drank in the company of men and, even more daring, talked about Freud and passion and sex. It was not that women actually behaved that way but the new styles reflected their aspirations. They were reacting against the Victorian prudery of an older generation and against the taboos of their parents, in an age when the automobile gave a new-found freedom and when prosperity encouraged frivolity.

The styles of the 1930s suggested quite another image of womanhood. Dresses lengthened early in the decade and only rose to just below the knees by 1939. The natural waistline reappeared and the existence of breasts was acknowledged. Indeed, naïve men who remembered the 1920s might have thought a new anatomical species had emerged, with so many womanly curves in evidence. But this was not a reversion to the Victorian or Edwardian mother. There was no return to prim prudery, no passive submission to male dominance. The advertisements of the 1930s usually depicted a pert, alert, responsible young miss, one who could face reality with wholesome innocence. The blasé and sophisticated flapper of the 1920s had been replaced by the girl next door.

The female of the advertisements also had her counterpart in the world of entertainment. North American youth now had a special place on the movie screens across North America. The Andy Hardy series began in the 1930s. There was also Shirley Temple, the symbol of the innocent purity of childhood, cinematic proof that all was well in a world in which people could be poor but noble. Indeed, one of the striking features of the films of that era was their escapism. The film world is always a fantasy world but the form it takes reveals a great deal about the period. In our day the emphasis is on sexual liberation; in the 1930s moviegoers escaped by indulging vicariously in romance rather than love. There was almost no attempt to depict the harsh life of the 1930s. Walt Disney's *Snow White and the Seven Dwarfs* transported audiences to a never-never land of illusion. For adults there was the world of adventure, uncomplicated by social or psychological insights—with Gary Cooper, Clark Gable, Myrna Loy and Carole Lombard—an ethereal world where Fred Astaire could dance in tails beside a floodlit swimming pool and in which the fearless always won the fair. Moviegoers shared vicariously in the deeds of deering-do or of saccharine romance with the heroines available for a chaste embrace at the happy ending.

Radio programs also provided an escape from reality. Amos 'n' Andy was the most popular North American program at the beginning of the decade and by 1939 Edgar Bergen and Charlie McCarthy had significantly reduced the attendance at Sunday evening church services. Canadians had their own Happy Gang and their Hockey Night in Canada with Foster Hewitt, but in cultural terms these were merely regional forms of the kinds of programs broadcast across North America.

Popular magazines followed the same pattern. The *Saturday Evening Post* and *Reader's Digest* prospered during the 1930s. The recipe was reassuring optimism with old-fashioned virtues bringing happiness or wealth. Again Canadians had their own mass-circula-tion magazines—*Maclean's*, *Chatelaine* and *Canadian Home Journal*—but there was much the same mixture of romantic fiction, biographies of success and helpful hints for blissful family life. The harsh realities of the depression were carefully excluded.

Even the major news items of the decade, those which held the interest of newspaper readers for week after week, suggest escapism. The Lindbergh kidnap-ping gave readers glimpses into the private life of an American hero and at the same time let them share vicariously in a personal tragedy. Then there was the abdication of Edward VIII. What could be more ro-mantic than a king—a constitutional monarch, it is true, but a king nonetheless—who would risk his throne for love, and for the love of a commoner at that? At first Canadian newspapers were more circumspect than their American counterparts. They only gave full rein to the gossip about Mrs. Simpson after the affair had been referred to in the English press. There was no such restraint for the Dionne quintuplets, however, and it seemed that their every breath and whimper made the headlines and sold newspapers. Even the gangsters of the era were almost romantic figures, with John Dillinger robbing banks and shooting it out with the F.B.I. like the outlaws of frontier days.

Nonetheless it was possible to see differences be-tween Canadians and Americans even at the level of this mass culture. Canadians certainly believed that they were different. A survey of Canadian attitudes in the period shows that many Canadians believed that Americans were more materialistic, more violent and more degenerate. The typical American, in Canadian eyes at least, was brash and arrogant, with little re-spect for law and order and even less respect for the sanctity of marriage. This tells us little of what Americans were really like but it tells us a great deal about what Canadians thought of themselves. They singled out these aspects of American society because they believed that, by contrast, they compared favourably in these areas. In other words, they thought of themselves as more modest than Americans, more law-abiding and more committed to a stable matrimonial and family life.

There is no statistical proof that Canadians were right when they made these comparisons. What they believed is, nevertheless, significant. The image they had of themselves exerted subtle pressures for social conformity. It is also noteworthy that the qualities which seemed to distinguish Canadians—and to reveal their superiority—were qualities which clearly reflected conservative attitudes. The emphasis was on respect for traditional institutions—the courts, the legislatures, marriage, the family. Rugged individualism was not necessarily seen as a sin but it was clearly tempered by the values associated with social institutions and social conformity. Of course Canada also had riots and divorces and gun-toting criminals in the 1930s, and Canadians may have exaggerated their respect for order and decorum. But their social values were different, at least in degree.

The signs of a cautious attitude towards social change can be found in many places. A book on Canadian etiquette written in the 1930s makes the point directly. The author explains that English etiquette is not appropriate because Canadians are North Americans but that American rules are not appropriate either because Canadians are more conservative. Judging by this book, Canadian society was very proper indeed. Take smoking, for example:

Smoking by guests when in the dining-room of a

house is unheard of. Unless invited to smoke by the host or hostess, no one should ever light a cigarette or ask permission to do so at the table.[1]

A comment on bachelor dinners also suggests that the middle class in Canada were very stuffy about the behaviour of young ladies.

The bachelor, who has spacious enough apartments or who has his own home, may give formal dinners from time to time. Such a one naturally likes to make some kind of return for the hospitality he has enjoyed. A sister or woman relative may be asked to chaperon his parties...or a married woman friend may take the part of hostess.[2]

If Canadians actually followed these rules of etiquette, their manners were certainly genteel.

The contrast with American society was not restricted to rules of etiquette. The schools in Canada also appear to have been different. Outside of Quebec, the educational system resembled the American pattern: free schooling at the elementary and secondary level, compulsory attendance, usually to the age of sixteen, and a trend towards a wider choice of technical and vocational programs in the high schools. Within these similar systems, however, both the philosophy of education and the subject matter show marked differences.

In the United States "progressive education" had carried the day and was accepted by most influential educators. Progressive education was not easy to define. It was a reaction against the traditional emphasis on academic subjects, memory work, strict discipline

[1]G. Pringle, *Etiquette in Canada* (Toronto, 1932), p. 166.
[2]*Ibid.*, p. 161.

and the assumption that only the gifted few could be educated. It stressed training for citizenship rather than scholarship, and encouraged practical subjects, creative activities, student initiative. The school was seen as a social environment instead of an academic institution. Much of this was mere cant, hardly going beyond the jargon of "personality development," "creative self-expression" and "real-life experiences." Many teachers and community leaders paid lip-service to progressive ideas without putting them into practice. Nonetheless they did not challenge the assumptions of progressive education.

Canadian educators were not unresponsive to these new ideas. Curriculum changes were introduced in almost all the English-speaking provinces, and the influence of progressive ideas is quite apparent. There was much talk of group enterprises and class projects, in which the students would learn to plan together and to cooperate and so imbibe the principles of democratic living. The contrast with the present is startling. The approved theory of our day puts the stress on the uniqueness of the individual. A student should be encouraged to pursue his own interests, do "his own thing." In the 1930s the emphasis was on group activities, with students learning to cooperate, to conform. There was a great deal of talk about "education for democracy" but the context made it obvious that this meant accepting the decisions of the group and contributing to group goals.[3]

Even the leading Canadian educators, however, were only partial converts to progressive education. J.G. Althouse, principal of the Ontario College of Education, for example, believed in the child-centred class-

[3]See, for example, the Programmes of Studies for Ontario as revised in 1938.

room but he also believed that learning was the product of discipline and hard work. He could applaud the concern for personality while continuing to stress the importance of teaching traditional subjects such as the classics.[4] There was no cult of novelty, no attempt to reject the past and to use the schools to create a completely new society.

This conservatism was even more marked in French Canada. Indeed, progressive education had almost no impact there. The French-language school system had no equivalent to the high schools in the rest of Canada. French Canadians who wanted their children to go beyond elementary school had to send them to residential classical colleges, where the curriculum was still based on Greek and Latin, and where priests distributed prizes or punishments untroubled by the ideas of John Dewey or Sigmund Freud.

The subject matter in Canadian schools also suggests a respect for inherited traditions. Canada may have been a North American country but Canadian students spent little time on the history or the institutions of the United States. Even the history of Canada was not taught as national history but as part of the history of the British Empire. The emphasis was on British traditions and British institutions; the American myth of a new and unfettered society in the new world never appeared in Canadian textbooks. The "love of freedom, justice and democracy" came, not from the frontier, but from the Mother of Parliaments.[5]

It is dangerous to read too much into Department of Education guidelines and school curricula, since official pronouncements may have little effect on classroom teachers. Nor can it be assumed, even if new

[4]J.G. Althouse, *Addresses* (Toronto, 1958).
[5]See the Ontario Programme of Studies for Grades VII and VIII, 1938.

attitudes and teaching methods are adopted, that when the children grow up they will be so very different from their parents. The school, after all, is only one of many influences on the young, and what they learn at home or on the street may be more important in the long run. These statements nonetheless do show what many Canadians thought the schools should be doing in the 1930s. Obviously they did not believe in drastic social change, in trying to build a new world by rejecting the heritage of the past.

Canadian universities were, if anything, even more strongly committed to hallowed traditions. In the United States universities, and especially the state universities, were responding to the demands of an industrial society by teaching a wide range of professional and technical skills. This utilitarian approach had its critics, but it was clearly dominant during this decade. The federal government during the depression actually subsidized needy university students in order "to extend the educational opportunities of the youth of the country and to bring them through the processes of training into the possession of skills which enable them to find employment."[6] Canadian universities, on the other hand, still shuddered at the idea that universities should stress vocational training. Even the National Research Council—originally established to foster industrial research in Canada—was arguing in 1938 that it should be concerned with pure research, untainted by any "immediate utilitarian objectives."[7]

---

[6]E.L. Kandel, *American Education in the Twentieth Century* (Boston, 1957), p. 52.

[7]N.R.C. submission to Royal Commission on Dominion Provincial Relations, cited in *A Science Policy For Canada,* Report of Senate Special Committee on Science Policy, Volume I (Ottawa, 1970), p. 49.

This ivory-tower approach was being challenged by some social scientists. The trend was more obvious in the United States where many lawyers, economists and political scientists became deeply involved in the problems of the depression. The New Deal policies were to a large extent the product of academics who formed Roosevelt's "Brains Trust." In Canada a few professors felt a similar urge to serve society directly but the older political parties were not very receptive to new ideas. The new socialist party did have the League for Social Reconstruction as its equivalent of a Brains Trust. The professors in this League, however, were shunned or bitterly criticized by their academic colleagues for stooping to politics. Even the fact that the L.S.R. was directly modelled on the British Fabian Society was no protection. Canadian universities were so committed to the ivory tower that two professors at McGill—Eugene Forsey and King Gordon—lost their jobs because of their political activity and Frank Underhill's professorship at the University of Toronto was in jeopardy.

The differences between education in Canada and the United States in the 1930s did not prove that there was a distinctive Canadian society emerging. It could have been that Canadians were merely lagging behind, that given time they would catch up to the progressive and utilitarian outlook of the United States. This argument rests on the unstated assumption that there was only one possible social pattern in North America. As Canada became more urbanized and more industrialized, so the argument went, it would imitate the American way of life. The uniformity of mass culture in North America—of styles and popular entertainment—seemed to support this view. Canada was different only because it was backward. Time, it was argued, would irresistibly erode the differences.

This argument becomes less convincing if we look at what Canadian writers were saying in the 1930s. Canadian novelists were not explicit about Canadian identity but the differences between Canadian and American novelists is nonetheless suggestive. Canadians, like Americans, were reading historical romances such as *Anthony Adverse* and *Gone with the Wind*. In the United States, however, social protest became a distinguishing feature of the literature of the 1930s. The Lost Generation of the 1920s, the expatriates who had washed their hands of middle-class Babbittry, was followed by a generation committed to political reform. Many of them found their model in Soviet Russia; Upton Sinclair after a visit to Moscow, could proclaim that "I have seen the future and it works." Morley Callaghan, the best Canadian novelist of the decade, was also appalled by the depression. He found his heroes and heroines among the poor and the alienated and he portrayed their lives with realism and sensitivity. But Callaghan did not write proletarian literature in the Marxist sense. He was more concerned with individual morality than with the class struggle.

The best French-Canadian novel of the decade, Philippe Panneton's *Trente Arpents*, fits into the same pattern. It is a novel of rural rather than of urban society, with the thirty-acre farm dominating the lives of the Moisan family. Again, however, there is the focus on poor people, burdened by the depression, human beings but certainly not heroes of the proletariat. Canadian novelists, it would seem, were too conscious of social continuity and the strength of traditions and institutions to commit themselves to the idea of social revolution.

Historians of the 1930s were much more specific about the nature of Canadian identity. Their analysis was an explicit affirmation that Canadian society had qualities which clearly distinguished it from American society. Until the 1930s, Canadian historians had concentrated on the development of Canada from colony to Dominion. In the 1930s the attention shifted to Canada as an entity in its own right. Canada, as they saw it, was not a new society, freed from the bonds of a decadent Europe. Harold Innis, in *The Fur Trade in Canada*, saw the separate existence of modern Canada foreshadowed by the fur-trading empire which spread across the northern half of the continent in the eighteenth century. Donald Creighton, in *The Commercial Empire of the St. Lawrence*, saw transportation on the St. Lawrence and the Great Lakes as the basis of a separate northern economy until the mid-nineteenth century. The conclusion was that Canada's separate political existence had its roots in a separate and distinctive economy in North America. An essential part of this thesis was that this economy linked Canada closely to Europe and especially to Great Britain. Canada, economically, politically and socially, was thus an extension of the old world in the new; not a pale image of a more advanced American society, but a unique combination of European and North American influences. Canadian society, so the thesis ran, was firmly based on institutions and traditions which had their origins in Europe.

The historians were probably right. Canadians of the 1930s did seem to have a greater respect for social stability. They did not accept the myth of a new society in the new world. French Canadians probably had more respect for inherited traditions than did English Canadians and, within English Canada, easterners may have been more conservative than westerners. If we may risk the generalization, however, it does appear that Canadian society was more securely founded on the heritage of the past than was the society of the United States. This was more than a difference of degree or stage of development; Canadian society was a new species.

It was still possible that the decade of the 1930s would crumble these foundations. The vast majority of Canadians, as we have seen, adopted American styles, watched American films, listened to American radio programs and read American periodicals and books. Constant exposure might erode whatever indigenous characteristics they had. It was also true that Canada was becoming more urban and more industrial. It was still possible that an industrial society would create or mold appropriate institutions, eliminating even the vestiges of the traditions of an earlier society. Instead of redressing the balance, the new world might supplant the old, even in Canada.

And then there was the depression. The depression was more than a down-swing of the business cycle; it was a decade of continuing economic disaster. To some it seemed a permanent affliction. Not surprisingly, many Canadians lost confidence in institutions which had permitted—or had perhaps even caused—this economic collapse. The traditions which Canadians had respected would certainly be questioned and challenged. The idea of a radically new society might well look more attractive, given the abysmal failure of the old. Whatever Canadian society may have been at the beginning of the decade, the depression ensured that it would never be quite the same again.

2
The Personal Impact of the Depression

In retrospect the depression appears as an unmitigated disaster, a decade of impotent despair in which people could only wait helplessly for the return of better days. It was not quite like that. The impact of the depression differed by region, by community and even by family. Some men never lost their jobs; on some farms the rain still fell. Even for the most fortunate, however, the depression left its mark. Nobody lived through the decade of the 1930s without some scars.

It must be remembered that a depression is something more than an economic recession, something more than statistics on unemployment, on gross national product, on freight loadings, on interest rates and investments. Statistics are important but they tell little about what the depression really meant to Canadians. A depression is really a state of mind, a loss of faith in stability and security. It may come early for some people. In the slums of Montreal and North Winnipeg there were families even in the 1920s whose only income was welfare payments, families for whom poverty and hopelessness were inescapable and normal. For such families there had always been a depression, and the 1930s was worse only because it was more widespread and the competition for welfare services was greater. On the other hand, there were some families whose income was not significantly affected by the depression—people on salaries who never lost their jobs. Annual salary increases were unheard of, and most wage-earners took a cut in salary at some time during the decade, but the cost of food and the cost of housing dropped, and in terms of real income those who kept their jobs were often better off in these years.

But even these fortunate people did not escape unscathed. It was impossible to live in Canada without absorbing the depression mentality. No matter how secure a person might be there were always relatives or friends whose plight brought home the reality of the depression. And no matter how secure a job might be there was always some apprehension; businesses which had once seemed as solid as the Precambrian Shield were going bankrupt. Wage-earners were aware that in the ranks of the unemployed there were men who could probably replace them and would be delighted to do so at half the salary. Couple this with the growing pessimism as hard times continued year after year, with the fear that things could and would get worse, and it is easier to understand why the survivors still remember.

In this sense the depression is still with us. Any Canadian over the age of forty-five remembers something about those years, and the sense of insecurity may never be completely dispelled. The realization that disaster can strike instills a caution which still survives. Young people today are often willing to quit one job before they find another or to interrupt their formal education for a year of travel; they argue that there are more important things than steady employment and that there is no hurry to leap onto the treadmill of a career. Their parents, on the other hand, are likely to be uneasy until their children have given hostages to fortune and have the stability that comes with sick leave, pension rights and all the other trimmings of economic security. We tend to assume that this generation gap is inevitable; that age is synonymous with caution. There may be some truth in this but the heritage of the depression is a factor. The gap is widened when parents brought up in the 1930s have children who have lived their lives in a more affluent era.

The impact, however, was greatest on two large groups in Canada: the unemployed and the prairie farmer. For both of these groups the depression was a tragic experience which tested their fortitude and shattered their comfortable illusions about Canadian society and Canadian institutions. Both for the unemployed and the farmers the initial problem was the simple, the obvious, the stark necessity of keeping themselves and their families alive. This in itself brought home to them the instability and fragility of what had once seemed ordered lives. It was not their fault; they were not to blame if the factory closed down or the drought shrivelled their crops. And yet, if they were to eat they had to rely on handouts. Their first requirement was charity. Without an income, they had to rely on somebody else to provide food, clothes and shelter.

Even if survival was assured, the problems of the depression were not resolved. Charity is too cold and too unreliable to be easily accepted as a way of life. To be kept alive was only the beginning; the unemployed wanted jobs and the farmers wanted to make an honest living. There could be no security until the depression ended and until there was some confidence that it would not return. A return to the good old days was not enough; the good old days had culminated in disaster. For many, the conclusion was that Canadian institutions and Canadian society would have to be changed. The 1930s was thus more than a period of economic recession. It was also a time when Canadians seriously, and almost for the first time, began to analyse the structure of their society and the role of social institutions. They questioned the accepted values in political and economic life, and debated radical ideas which only a few years before would have been ridiculed as utopian or heretical.

This questioning came later. The first problem for many was to keep alive. For the man who lost his job the immediate need was food. With no income and a family to feed, what could a man do? In most cases the awareness of disaster came slowly. Losing a job was not the end of the world, and the first and natural step was to look for another. It was hard to realize that there might not be a job; it was part of the Canadian myth that there was always work for men who wanted to work. So the family would live on its savings, or borrow money from relatives, or get an extension of credit at the corner grocery store, while the husband read the want-ads and tramped the streets to find a job. The competition was intense, and any advertisement in a newspaper would bring out block-long queues of eager applicants. Rumours about jobs circulated widely and even rumours had to be taken seriously; men had to be at the front of the line if they were to have any chance at all. Around construction jobs there was often a group of unemployed men waiting—on the off chance that the foreman would fire somebody and hire one of them on the spot to take over the shovel or hammer.

But the harsh reality could not be ignored for long. For most of the unemployed there were no jobs and there would be no jobs. It was all very well to talk about self-reliance and initiative, about fortitude and tightening belts, but virtue does not fill empty stomachs. Eventually the jobless found themselves with no more savings and no more credit. All that was left for them was to go on relief.

For most Canadians to go on relief was a humiliating experience. There was a deep-rooted feeling that to accept charity—especially charity from the state—was a confession of failure. It was a question of self-respect, of personal pride, a reflection of North American individualism, a relic of a simpler society when men could support themselves if they had the will and the strength. It was also an attitude which had been strengthened by suspicious and parsimonious officials, dating back to the Elizabethan Poor Law, when indigents were treated as slackers and were punished for being poor. Canadian society still shared the belief that a man who could not manage his own affairs was incompetent or lazy.

This attitude was obviously archaic in an industrial society in the 1930s. It was impossible to believe that all the unemployed were to blame for their unfortunate plight. Governments recognized that they were dealing with a new phenomenon. To avoid the stigma of charity, most relief recipients signed a form promising when good times returned to pay for the relief they received. But this nod to self-respect was no more than a futile gesture. The stigma of accepting charity had outlived its relevance but it was still alive, and very real, both for men on relief and for officials who administered relief. Add to this sentiment the desperate efforts of municipal, provincial and federal governments to avoid bankruptcy, with the imperative of limiting the size of the relief rolls, as well as the usual impersonal and incredible red tape of bureaucracy, and it is easy to understand that to be on relief remained a humiliating experience. To be on the dole was to be something less than human in the Canada of the 1930s.

For a man driven by desperation the first step was to get on the relief rolls. Forms had to be filled out and an investigator had to make sure that the family really was penniless—a degrading beginning. If there were complications, such as a dependent parent, more forms would be required. Finally the family was declared eligible.

The ways in which food was distributed varied from one city to the next. Some cities issued food directly from a city depot. In this way the city could economize by bulk purchases of basic foods. It meant, however, that each family, whether it was Irish, Italian or Ukrainian, was expected to eat the same food. It also meant that local merchants soon had no customers. The more usual arrangement involved vouchers which could be exchanged in grocery stores for foods which appeared on an approved list. For a family of four the vouchers might come to a total of $4 or $5 a week. This was hardly generous, but it did not mean starvation when bread was 4 cents a loaf and eggs were 15 cents a dozen.

Food, of course, was only a beginning. Families had to have a roof over their heads and in winter they had to heat their homes. There were other vouchers covering rent and fuel, again with forms to fill out and with inspections to make sure that nobody was cheating. Over the years clothes often became the most serious problem of all. In the first year or two it was assumed that the depression was a temporary emergency; people were expected to make do with the clothes they had. As the years passed the clothing situation became more and more serious, especially for children. Churches and other charitable agencies collected and distributed carloads of used clothing for those on relief but even so a voucher system for clothing eventually had to be introduced. There was little concern for style or quality. It was something to be clad and shod.

The basic necessities were thus provided—at least the minimum for survival. It was often the small items that created the most inconvenience. James Gray in his reminiscences of the depression in Winnipeg describes the frustration of never having money for razor blades, needles, light bulbs or for a movie. Naturally there was no money for cigarettes or beer; no government was prepared to pay for indulging in such vices. The only cash that a family saw came from odd jobs or temporary employment, and even this was likely to be deducted from relief vouchers if it became known. People survived but for many the depression was a period of bitter frustration, of degradation, made more human only by the comradeship and sympathy of others who shared the same problems, the same resentments and the same faith that somehow the depression would end.

The obvious question, in retrospect, is why the unemployed were not usefully employed on public works. Why not pay wages instead of relief and have something to show for it in the form of schools, parks and roads? The unemployed would have their self-respect and Canadian society would benefit from their efforts. The advantages of relief projects were so obvious that even in the 1930s every government talked about providing useful employment for those who were out of work. The difficulty was the cost. Wages are only a portion of the total cost of construction projects; expenditure on equipment and machinery is usually as high as the amount paid out to workers. The harsh fact was that governments could not afford to create employment. Even the direct relief payments bankrupted many municipalities and provinces. How could the city of Montreal or the province of Saskatchewan undertake increased expenditures when at some times almost half of the population was on relief and, of course, couldn't pay taxes. Some projects were undertaken, projects in which manual labour was the major input. But such schemes did not accomplish much, and there was a tendency to use shovels instead of bulldozers, handsaws instead of power saws, just to make work. For most men on relief there was usually nothing to do, and if there was organized work it was likely to be what became known as "boondoggles"—raking leaves, digging dandelions, shovelling snow—work which in the long run was unproductive and certainly not very stimulating. Relief remained what it had been from the beginning: handouts to tide people over the depression.

The plight of the farmers was much different; they were not unemployed. They tilled their fields, sowed their grain, hoed their gardens, did their chores, much as they had done before the depression. What was changed was that in the 1930s the bottom had fallen out of the market for the goods they produced. Wheat, which had been $2 a bushel for some years in the 1920s, plummeted until in 1932 it was 34 cents a bushel —the lowest recorded price in three hundred years. Indeed, after the cost of seeding and harvest, farmers lost money on every bushel they produced. Nor was it only wheat. Beef, milk, eggs: every item of farm produce was worth only a fraction of what it had brought a few years before. Here for example is an extract from a letter written by a Saskatchewan farmer to Charles Dunning in the spring of 1932.

Eggs in Broadview 6¢. My sister took in 75 dozen yesterday and it took a third of the money she got to buy a ¼ lb. tin of mustard and there you are. But to hell with kicking, Charlie, both of us are alright. We got no relief and therefor no "caveeats" and if our grub aint too good we are still as independent as ever. . . . We go ahead from one experience to another, and in time will doubtless solve the greatest mystery of them all.[1]

The loss of income from falling prices was enough to create a real crisis on the prairies. Machinery had to be repaired or replaced if farming was to go on, and the prices of manufactured goods did not decline as much as the prices of farm products. At the same time most farmers had mortgages on their land, dating back to the 1920s, with interest rates at 6 or 7 per cent (a high at the time; rates fell in the 1930s to 3 and 4 per cent). It now took six bushels of wheat to repay as much interest as one bushel had repaid in better times, if a farmer had anything left over after he had paid for all the costs of seeding and harvest.

But what could the farmers do? Manufacturers in a similar situation had an alternative. They could limit production to balance supply and demand, and so stabilize the price of what they produced at a profitable level—which helps to explain why the price of manufactured goods was relatively stable. Farmers had no

[1]C.A. Dunning Papers, Joe Bird to C.A. Dunning, 1 May 1932.

choice. They were producing wheat for an international market over which they had no control. Even if an individual farmer restricted his production it would have no significant effect on the world wheat supply. All the farmer could do was to plant his wheat and hope for the best, hope that by fall the price would be better. And so he continued to put in his wheat every spring —wheat acreage fell only slightly in these years—and found at harvest time that he had made a mistake.

But this was only part of the story, and for most of the farmers on the prairies it was not the worst. The drop in farm prices was overshadowed by disasters which were not directly related to the depression. By a coincidence the 1930s were also years of natural disasters. First and foremost was the drought. The true prairies—the treeless flat lands of southern Saskatchewan which form the Palliser Triangle—had been settled since the turn of the century. Unsuspecting immigrants knew nothing of long-range weather cycles, and the probability of a prolonged dry period. They knew that they depended upon June rains and that the rains did not always come, but nothing had prepared them for a succession of dry years and therefore complete crop failures. Starting in 1929 in some areas, farmers planted their crops in the spring year after year, only to see them shrivel in the remorseless summer heat. By 1931 and 1932 soil conditions had become worse and spring winds became dust storms, sometimes carrying away topsoil and seed. As a child I can remember watching light cumulus clouds in the sky— everybody watched the sky—wondering if the clouds would thicken and darken and bring us rain. I also vividly remember one hot day, when suddenly we became aware of the close hush that precedes a sudden thunderstorm. Instead we saw on the horizon a long low black crescent moving toward us, bringing dust instead of rain. It passed quickly, but it left behind a heavy layer of dust on everything, inside the house as well as outside.

I can remember, too, looking up towards the sun to see thousands of tiny flecks of white above me. These were the grasshoppers, which some years cut off the cereal crops before the sun could do its damage, but which also ate the grass in the pastures and the leaves off all the garden plants. Yet another recollection is in midsummer of 1935, commenting to my father with the confident wisdom of a ten-year-old boy that the crops were in wonderful condition—the rains came that year. With the pessimism of experience my father reluctantly agreed that things looked good but that the crops weren't harvested yet. They never were harvested, for that was the year of the rust, with rust spores cutting off all nourishment to the undeveloped heads of wheat. That year there was fodder for the livestock but little grain.

Conditions changed from year to year and from region to region. Outside the Palliser Triangle, in Manitoba, Alberta and northern Saskatchewan, rainfall was close to normal and at least hay could be grown for livestock and garden vegetables for the families. In some areas of southern Saskatchewan, however, there were nine successive years of almost total crop failures.

Farm relief was much more complex, and much more expensive, than unemployment relief. The basic problems of providing food, shelter and clothing were much the same; without any income, farmers were as dependent as urban dwellers on charity. But farmers were also in business. They could not wait patiently until they found a job. Farming was their job and they had to invest time and money each spring in the hope that conditions would improve. Some farmers gave up, deserted their mortgaged farms and migrated with their families to the cities, where they sheltered in tar-paper shacks and looked for work like the rest of the unemployed. Others loaded their remaining posses-sions in a farm truck or wagon and moved north where there was more chance of rain. But most of them stayed, held by hope, or by the fear that conditions elsewhere would be just as bad. And for these farmers, with al-most no income from the year before, the government had to go beyond subsistence relief; it had to finance their farming operations as well.

This form of farm relief accounts for two-thirds of the total relief expenditures in Saskatchewan in the 1930s. First of all there was seed grain; a bushel or so for every acre seeded. A crop failure the year before meant that the government had to supply the seed. Then there were repairs for farm machinery; seeding, ploughing and harvesting halted if the equipment broke down and the farmer couldn't replace broken parts. There was also fuel for the tractors or feed and fodder for the livestock. Hay had to be shipped into drought areas to keep farm animals alive over the win-ter; horses working in the fields in the spring also needed oats or barley to supplement their diet. Many cattle were sold or slaughtered for the farmer's own family, but some had to be kept for milk, and for breed-ing stock, and again feed and fodder had to be supplied. To farmers and governments alike it often seemed a fruitless and wasteful effort. Yet year after year the effort had to be made. The alternative was to give up—to admit final and complete defeat—to depopulate the prairies and wait for the buffalo and Indians to take over again.

The farmers were the major but not the only stricken people on the prairies. In most parts of Canada com-munities included both employed and unemployed, and the former paid enough in taxes to maintain many of the community services. On the prairies, however, the depression affected everybody. Entire areas were paralysed by the drought. Municipalities could collect no property taxes because nobody had money. Doctors and dentists could not live on their fees because their patients could not pay them; in Saskatchewan the provincial government paid doctors a monthly stipend to keep them in the drought areas. Municipalities could not pay teachers—not even the $400 a year which was the average salary. Instead, teachers were given relief vouchers so they could live, and they received the balance that was due to them in the form of a promissory note. Not surprisingly, many teachers left their profession in those years; the promissory notes were redeemed years later.

The unemployed and the prairies farmers were the largest groups on relief in the decade but there was another category of relief recipients which received special attention. These were the "single, homeless, unemployed." They were young men for the most part, with no jobs and no family ties, who often travelled from place to place, "riding the rods," looking for work, frequently begging for food wherever the freight trains stopped, and usually ending up by swelling the numbers of unemployed in the larger cities.

These men received special attention for two reasons. One was the concern for the future of young men who had never known security, had never had steady jobs, and who, it was feared, would be irreparably scarred physically and morally. After years as transients, would they ever be able to settle down and become responsible citizens? The fears may have been exaggerated but they were nonetheless genuine. The other reason for concern was the fear that these men were a danger to the established order. Men like Senator Robertson, Minister of Labour in the Bennett government, still frightened by the memories of the Winnipeg General Strike, were convinced that these men were potential revolutionaries and that many of them were already communists. Robertson's solution was to deport those who didn't have Canadian citizenship and to exile the rest in remote labour camps.

Labour camps were established in 1932 and for the next five years these camps contained an average of twenty thousand men. They were founded for mixed motives. They were seen in part as a means of providing useful employment and so preparing the men for a useful life of responsible citizenship after the depression ended. Thus the men were not conscripted but volunteered for the camps, and were paid the munificent sum of 20 cents a day—the federal government was not extravagant. The fear of revolution was also a factor; most camps were located in remote areas and were administered by the Department of National Defence. Any complainer, any man who organized a grievance committee to protest about the food or the discipline, was likely to be labelled a "Red," shipped out of the camp and listed as a dangerous agitator in the files of the R.C.M.P. Useful work was done by the men in these camps. Airfields were built in northern Quebec and northern Ontario and in British Columbia, and historic forts were restored in eastern Canada. Within a few years, however, the Department of National Defence began to run out of suitable projects and discipline became more repressive.

It was from some of the camps in British Columbia that the On-to-Ottawa trek began in 1935. A few hundred men boarded freight trains in Vancouver intending to protest directly to R. B. Bennett. Their numbers increased as they travelled east until the march was halted by the police at Regina. The men were held there in the Exhibition Grounds and weeks passed without incident. Bennett decided to act, however, and ordered the arrest of the leaders of the trek. The arrests provoked a riot in which one policeman was killed, although it never assumed serious proportions (or so it seems today, when we have become hardened to insurrections in which city blocks are devastated and the dead and wounded are counted in the tens or hundreds). Shortly after the riot the men agreed to disperse and returned to the camps or found their way to various cities. The camps themselves were closed by the Liberal government in 1936, with the railways agreeing to provide work at standard wages for most of the men.

The story of relief for the unemployed, for the farmers and the transients, is only the beginning of the history of Canada in the 1930s. Relief made physical survival possible. The depression did not lead to widespread starvation or death from exposure in Canada; the various levels of government kept people alive. But these men could not live by bread alone. For some of them ten long years passed without a job or without a crop. At first the depression could be borne because it seemed to be a temporary crisis, a passing phase. As time went by, however, many reacted against a continuing and seemingly endless dependence on relief. They could not believe that the riddle of the depression could not be resolved and they demanded action, effective action. And by action most of them meant political action. Governments had the power.

Relief was thus only the first step. Governments were expected to go further, to take control of the economic system and to direct it and manipulate it to bring an end to the depression. People might not agree on how this was to be done but they were sure it had to be done. And it is here, even more than in the economic effects of the depression, that the real heritage of the 1930s is to be found. It became an intensely political decade; a decade of political radicalism, of new concepts of the economic role of government, and of the creation of new political parties and new political institutions to apply these concepts in practice. To survive was not enough; men on relief wanted to live in a world in which relief would no longer be necessary.

3
The Depression as a Political Catalyst

The last century of Canadian history can be divided into two periods. The first period begins with Confederation, or even before, and lasts until after the First World War. This was when the nation was forged, when the northern half of a continent became a political and economic entity. The second period begins where the first ended but it has no terminal date; it is the modern era in which we are still living. It rests on the achievements of the first period but the focus has shifted. The central problems are those of a modern industrial society and the relations between regions, groups and individuals within this society. There is no precise turning point, no date which marks the end of one period and the beginning of the next—history is never precise. The decade of the 1930s, however, is clearly a watershed.

The first period was the era of the National Policy. In 1867, for all the talk about dominion from sea to sea, Canada was only a huddling together of four of the seven British colonies in northern North America. Within a decade the boundary of Canada had been extended to include Prince Edward Island on the east coast, the Canadian Shield to the north, the prairies and British Columbia to the west. For the next fifty years the major objective was to give some reality to this vast but artificial creation. The geographical expression had to be given a political and economic identity.

By the 1920s the National Policy had achieved these aims. Railways had been built to link the geographical regions of Canada; a protective tariff had fostered industrial growth within Canada; and immigration had peopled the prairies and provided the labour force in the cities of central Canada. Politicians, federal and provincial, had collaborated with railway-builders, industrialists and land speculators to create a nation. This era was coming to an end even before the depression. Canada had more railway mileage per capita than any other country in the world; manufacturers already depended on foreign in addition to domestic markets, and most of the arable lands were under cultivation. The ground work had been laid but new policies and new priorities were needed. Canadians adjusted slowly to the new situation. The depression accelerated this process of adjustment, not because it created the new problems but because it aggravated them and made it impossible to ignore them.

The Canada created by the National Policy was an industrial society. The days of the frontier were past. The shift had been from an agrarian to an industrial economy, from a rural to an urban society. Even the prairie farmers were an integral part of this modern world. They operated a commercial enterprise, investing in land and equipment, producing a commodity for the European market and buying their food and clothing with the money they received. The urban proletariat was even more obviously tied to an interdependent industrial economy. Modern Canada offered material rewards and conveniences far beyond the aspirations of earlier generations, both for farmers and workers, but it also meant less independence. Income depended on remote markets over which they had no control. Even at the best of times, there could be bad years or bad seasons.

What changes could be expected? The National Policy had created a national entity but there had been some unpleasant side-effects. Regional economic disparities had been aggravated; industrialization brought with it the conflict of interests between capital and labour; and the uneasy balance between French and English Canadians was disrupted. These changes, and the legitimate grievances associated with them, were sure to shift national priorities.

Although the depression did not create this situation, it did re-enforce the need for new national policies. It aggravated some of the social cleavages already emerging, it made many of the new grievances more acute, and it influenced the choice of political priorities. It is in this sense that the decade of the 1930s is both the end of one era and the beginning of another. It marks the concern with the problems with which we are still painfully familiar.

Regional differences offer a good illustration of the changing context of national policies. Canada has always been a political association of different regions; political decisions have always been compromises between conflicting regional interests. The decision to adopt a federal system of government was in itself a recognition of this regionalism. The first federal cabinet, and every subsequent cabinet, has been a coalition of regional representatives. The National Policy was a direct attempt to overcome the geographical barriers between the regions by building railways, with the tariff to encourage trade between the regions. Thus, from the beginning, regionalism dominated Canadian politics.

The National Policy did link the diverse regions more closely and to that extent it achieved its purpose. Closer economic ties, however, did not eliminate regional differences. Most Maritimers, for example, were convinced that their region was being exploited by Upper Canadians. They blamed the railways which charged high freight rates on goods going to and from the Maritimes. They blamed the tariff which forced them to buy manufactured goods from Ontario instead of the cheaper goods manufactured in the United States. They blamed the west, where the federal government spent so much money for settlement— money coming in part from Maritime taxes. Behind these complaints was the bitter knowledge that the Maritime region had not shared in the prosperity of other regions of Canada. The closer ties with the rest of Canada merely made the disparities more apparent and more irritating.

The National Policy was not entirely to blame. The Maritime region suffered from certain disadvantages for which politicians were not responsible. It did not have abundant natural resources and it was remote from raw materials and markets. The sense of grievance was nonetheless real. The Maritime Rights movement, a protest against federal policies, dominated Maritime policies in the 1920s. The federal government did appoint a royal commission and, following its recommendations, did increase federal subsidies to the Maritime governments and reduce railway freight rates in the Maritime region. But these were only palliatives, which helped but could not redress the balance between the Maritimes and the more prosperous regions of Canada. With the depression the economic grievances became more acute than ever. What was needed was a new national policy which would give Maritimers the feeling that they too could share in the benefits which other regions seemed to have derived from the federal union.

The prairie provinces was another region with grievances. The National Policy had built a web of railways across the prairies and brought settlers to make the land productive. Once this was accomplished, however, the disadvantages of the National Policy became more apparent. Westerners, like the Maritimers, objected to a federal tariff which forced them to buy agricultural machinery and cars built in Ontario when they could have been imported more cheaply from the United States. They complained of the freight rates on the long haul of goods to and from the prairies.

Prairie grievances also led to political action in the 1920s. Unlike the Maritimes, where the pressure was exerted within the Liberal and Conservative parties, the prairie farmers founded a new political party, the Progressive party. Again, however, this political agitation reflected the fact that the National Policy had achieved its purpose and that new political perspectives were required. As with the Maritimes, the focus was on regional economic disparities. The federal government responded—both tariffs and freight rates were lowered slightly. This was enough to satisfy the prairies for the moment; most of the Progressives had rejoined the Liberal party by the end of the decade. Again, however, this was only a palliative.

Juggling tariffs and freight rates would not be enough. The prairies had to sell their wheat on the world market. By the end of the 1920s the market was glutted. Wheat-producing countries—Canada, the United States, Argentina and Australia—had expanded their wheat acreage during and after the war to meet the European demand. European countries, however, had recovered from the war and had encouraged domestic production of grain by means of subsidies and tariffs. It was not long before more wheat was being grown than could be consumed. Even the crop failures in Canada in the 1930s did not eliminate the world surplus. With huge carry-overs of wheat from one year to the next, the price dropped from an average of over $1 a bushel in the 1920s to a low of 34 cents in 1932. The National Policy had no answer to this problem.

A new approach to regional disparities emerged during the 1930s. Special institutions, such as the Wheat Board, were created to control the marketing of Canadian exports. Far more important, however, was the new idea that the federal government should reduce disparities by giving larger subsidies to the provincial governments in the poorer regions. Simple and obvious as this may seem, it was really a very radical idea. It amounted to the proposal of a new and quite different national policy.

The old National Policy had been concerned with economic expansion, and the nation's economy had expanded although not all regions had benefited to the same degree. The new concept focused on the more equitable distribution of the national income. The argument was that comparable social services should be provided for every Canadian in whatever region he lived. A citizen, just because he was a Canadian, was assumed to have a right to the same level of government services, whether it was transporation, education or social welfare. Thus a boy living in Ecum Secum, Nova Scotia, or Moose Jaw, Saskatchewan, would be entitled to as good an education as a boy living in Toronto or Vancouver.

The idea gained support in the 1930s because the disparities in social services were so extreme, but it was still too radical a concept to win immediate acceptance. Equality is an admirable objective but what one person gains another may lose. In this case the poorer provinces would need more money—money that would have to come from the wealthier regions of the country. Taxes collected in Ontario would be spent in Prince Edward Island or Alberta. Not all Canadians were ready to accept responsibility for fellow citizens living in other regions. By the end of the 1930s, however, the idea had growing support and had even been enshrined in the report of the most important royal commission in our history—the Rowell-Sirois Report on Dominion-Provincial Relations. The concern for regional disparities underlies the equalization grants, the regional development schemes, and indeed many of the major reforms initiated in Canada over the last forty years.

Regional disparities were not the only economic disparities in Canada. The National Policy had fostered urbanization and industrialization in Canada. With industrialism came the problems of the urban wage-earner. A city worker may enjoy many amenities: regular hours, regular income, and the variety of a larger community. The urban family, however, bears little resemblance to a rural family. On a family farm children can make a direct economic contribution by doing chores and helping in many of the farm activities. Even old people can find a useful role. In the city only the wage-earner brings in money; children and elderly people become a financial burden who add nothing to the family income. Family allowances and old age pensions are a response to this change in family relationships. In industrial societies, governments have accepted some responsibility for those who earn nothing for themselves. It is no coincidence that old age pensions were first introduced in Canada in the 1920s, when industrialization was well advanced.

The economic instability of an industrial society, however, goes beyond the young and the old. In the 1930s the industrial machine slowed down and thousands of wage-earners lost their jobs. Without wages, families were destitute. As city-dwellers they could not even grow their own vegetables. It was only then that the precarious nature of industrial society became glaringly apparent, that able-bodied men, willing and eager to work, realized that, through no fault of their own, they could not support their families. There could be no turning back—the cities and factories were here to stay. The only solution was for society, meaning governments, to provide an income until men could once more find jobs.

Industrialism also brought with it the cleavage between labour and capital. The Winnipeg strike of 1919 was the first major clash in which the rhetoric of the class struggle was prominent. Trade union membership declined in the early years of the decade—working conditions and raises in pay were less important than finding jobs. By the end of the decade, however, there were portents of more militant activity. Industrial unionism emerged as a rival to the staid and traditional craft unionism of the Canadian Congress of Labour. Craft unions associated workers such as machinists and metal workers into separate unions, whereas industrial unions united all workers in the same industry and so made it possible for union leaders to speak for all workers when negotiating with

Ford or General Motors. Industrial unionism was the harbinger of a more class-conscious labour force, bent on finding its place in the sun. It was also anathema to industrial and mining magnates who saw the red flag and bloody revolution lurking in the wings. The major incident was the Oshawa strike, a strike which was settled peacefully but not before Premier Hepburn of Ontario had threatened to suppress the "communist" agitators by force. The great expansion in trade union membership only came with the war but the new structures and the greater awareness of the demands of labour had their beginnings in the 1930s.

To the divisions between regions and classes in Canada must be added the cultural division, the split between French and English Canadians. Industrialization would inevitably exacerbate French-English relations in Canada. It would break down the isolation of rural Quebec and bring French Canadians into direct and daily contact with the other culture. The fact that this contact usually took the form of English-Canadian bosses and foremen giving orders to French-Canadian workers only made matters worse.

There was no open clash between the wars because no French-Canadian champion emerged who spoke for these workers. The French-Canadian elites felt menaced, not only by the English-speaking and Protestant majority in Canada, and indeed in North America, but also by the new and alien ideas associated with industrialization—radical ideas which were usually labelled socialism or communism. The traditional leaders of French Canada offered no answers to the new problems of an industrial society. Their response was essentially negative. They saw any change as a threat to French-Canadian survival and stressed more than ever the traditional bulwarks of *la survivance*: language, religion and provincial autonomy. There were some

French-Canadian separatists in the 1930s but they too were reacting against the changes within Quebec. They turned their backs on the twentieth century and offered instead a utopian vision of an idyllic French, Catholic and rural Laurentia. Industrialism might have been a cultural powder-keg if aggressive French-Canadian leaders had appeared. The fuse would only be lit in the 1950s by the young intellectuals of *Cité Libre*—Pierre Trudeau, Gérard Pelletier and others. Only then would French Canadians begin to come to terms with modern industrial society and see survival in terms of controlling rather than rejecting modern institutions.

This meant that during the 1930s few English-Canadians were even aware that cultural conflict was imminent. French Canada had turned in on itself after the bitter rupture over conscription in 1917. Maurice Duplessis, who came to power in 1936, was denounced by English-Canadian liberals for his corrupt practices and authoritarian measures but they paid little attention to the broader problem of French-Canadian survival. Duplessis himself was not an aggressive nationalist. His support came from the traditional institutions of rural French Canada; his policy for survival came to little more than resisting federal initiatives. Camillien Houde, *le p'tit gars de Ste-Marie*, did speak for the urban proletariat in Montreal. Houde unfortunately was a demagogue on the make and was bought off by the vested interests before he created any trouble. The potential for a cultural explosion was there but few Canadians realized this in the 1930s.

In retrospect, then, we can see that the decade was a turning point. A creative period of Canadian history had come to an end. The National Policy had built a transcontinental nation with an integrated and industrialized economy. A new era had begun, the emergence of modern Canada, in which new institutions and new policies would be initiated in order to cope with the problems created by this national economy. Attention was shifting from the frontier to the metropolis, from the challenge of geography to the tensions between regions, classes and cultures. It would have been a period of controversy and confrontation even without an economic crisis. The depression had the effect of increasing the economic disparities and so increasing the tensions and divisions within Canadian society. It acted as a catalyst, accelerating the process of social adjustment.

It was also a pre-eminently political decade. Politics was seen as the means by which society would be changed; political leaders were seen as the natural agents of social reform. Some politicians from an earlier era managed to survive by adapting to the new situation. Most of the prominent politicians, however, emerged during the decade. They were new leaders promising new policies. In a sense most of them were failures. Their reforms were marginal; their careers were often brief. They were significant, however, because they represented the first attempts to meet the problems of an industrial Canada. Through their careers it is possible to see something of the fears, the hopes and the visions of the Canadians of those years. It is also possible to learn something about the Canada of today because the problems these men faced are still with us.

4

R. B. Bennett:
The Business Executive
in Politics

"MY GOVERNMENT"

Dale jumped at a peculiar, uncommon phrase used by Mr. Bennett in a speech, wherein he referred to "My Government," a phrase usually reserved for the King. Dale's happy inspiration reflected a belief which in 1935 is widely held, that Canada had acquired a One Man Show. (Jan. 19, 1931.)

R. B. Bennett is one of the least known of our prime ministers. He was active in Canadian politics for twenty years, leader of the Conservative party for ten and prime minister for five—from 1930 to 1935. And yet what mark has he left? For those who lived through the 1930s, he is mainly identified with the depression, as if he was to blame. His name is not linked with any great issue but with "Bennett buggies"—those symbols of the depression, cars with the engine removed, drawn by horses because the owner could not afford gasoline or repairs. Bennett's critics were virulent in their assessment of the man and his policies. J.W. Dafoe of the *Winnipeg Free Press*, for example, saw no good in this high-tariff Tory:

Mr. Bennett [he wrote] is not a great man. I think Laski hit him off very neatly when he said he was a little man with a big manner. It is perhaps fortunate that his talents are limited because with his delusions of grandeur and his various obsessions he would certainly wreck this country if his abilities matched his ambitions.[1]

Bennett had few defenders; even his colleagues felt no affection for him. He could be an arrogant bully. His cabinet ministers were rarely consulted on major policies and their opinions carried little weight. One of the stories going the rounds in the 1930s was of the tourist who saw R.B. Bennett walking alone towards Parliament Hill from his suite in the Château Laurier, talking to himself. He asked a bystander who it was and got the reply that it was the Prime Minister holding a cabinet meeting. Bennett dominated his government and his party while in office, and when the party was shattered and defeated he was loaded with all the blame.

Lord Beaverbrook was one of his apologists. Beaverbrook had been a friend and business associate since their childhood in New Brunswick. Bennett, he wrote:

...succeeded in saving his own country in that deadly season of peril. He gave supreme leadership in the face of disaster. His courage never faltered, his confidence never failed. He carried out unprecedented remedial measures, thus avoiding grievous damage which would have been inflicted upon the whole financial structure of the country.

In truth, I am convinced that no other man but Bennett would have had the courage to guide the shattered fortunes of Canada along uncharted waters of finance, and through unexplored forests of industry. He was bold, yet wise, he was determined, yet patient. He was a man.[2]

[1]J.W. Dafoe Papers, J.W. Dafoe to Grant Dexter, October 19, 1932.
[2]Lord Beaverbrook, *Friends* (London, 1959), p. 81.

Lord Beaverbrook is not an impartial witness. And yet there is much to be said on the credit side of Bennett's record in office. He created new institutions, institutions such as the Bank of Canada and the C.B.C., both of which represent a remarkable extension of government activity and both of which, in their own way, have been significant in shaping the Canadian nation. Under Bennett also, Canada endowed itself with outstanding civil servants, men such as Clifford Clark, Graham Towers and Donald Gordon, men who shaped our public service for a generation.

But there is a debit side too. As a politician he was a failure. He left the Conservative party leaderless and divided; he accentuated the divisions within the body politic—east versus west, capital versus labour, English versus French. Part of his legacy was the establishment of regional protest parties, the C.C.F. and Social Credit. However, when one draws up his balance sheet as a Canadian statesman, it is clear that he made an impact. Under R.B. Bennett the country underwent significant changes.

Bennett was chosen as party leader at the Conservative convention of 1927, to succeed Arthur Meighen. He came from a New Brunswick family, fallen on hard times. He taught school, saved money to take law at Dalhousie University and after a few years of practice moved to join a law firm in Calgary. He became a successful corporation lawyer, but was even more successful in investments in various corporation mergers (along with his friend Max Aitken, later Lord Beaverbrook). He had been active in politics provincially and federally and in 1927 agreed to dedicate himself entirely to politics. Bennett was fond of words like dedication and mission; he was brought up as a Bible-reading Methodist and his first public speeches had been made as a youth in the cause of temperance. Now at the age of fifty-seven he committed himself to the cause of conservatism in Canada.

It was not a propitious time for a Conservative crusade. In western Canada the agitation against the National Policy—and especially the tariffs—was so intense that it had given rise to a protest movement, the Progressives, in rebellion not only against the protectionist Conservative party but even against the more moderate tariff policy of the Liberals. By 1926 Mackenzie King had lured some Progressives back into the Liberal fold but the Conservatives had never recovered; Bennett was the only Conservative elected on the prairies in that year. One of his obvious tasks was to regain prairie support. The other Conservative problem was Quebec, where the heritage of conscription had left the party with no French-Canadian leader and few French-Canadian votes.

In many ways Bennett was ill-prepared to improve the party fortunes in either region. As far as the prairies was concerned, a corporation lawyer (especially one who had been western solicitor for the C.P.R.), a millionaire, and a champion of protective tariffs was highly suspect. As for Quebec, Bennett was known as an imperialist who had supported conscription. It was hard to imagine that he could win the confidence of voters in either region. And yet, three years after succeeding to the Conservative leadership, in the election of 1930 his party won 23 seats in the prairies and 25 seats in Quebec, and on the strength of these gains R.B. Bennett became Prime Minister of Canada.

This surprising achievement was not a miracle. For one thing, the increase in the popular vote for the Conservatives in these regions was not as great as the increase in elected members suggests. Only a relatively small percentage increase in the popular vote was needed to account for the spectacular gains in the number of seats. It was, nonetheless, a startling recovery for the party. The explanation lies in a combination of changing economic conditions and the personality of R.B. Bennett, the new party leader.

The world-wide depression was only beginning by the fall of 1930 and almost nobody realized how long or how serious it would be. Canadian bankers and manufacturers were still pointing out reassuringly that Canada's natural resources were unimpaired and that the demand for Canadian goods would soon reassert itself. Mackenzie King had known that unemployment was unusually severe in 1930 but he too assumed that the slack in the economy would soon be taken up. There was uneasiness but there was no panic. The Liberal government at Ottawa, however, was vulnerable because it seemed to be denying that there was any cause for concern.

Bennett's campaign, on the other hand, was marvellously appropriate at this conjuncture. He had started campaigning with tremendous vigour immediately after the Conservative convention. His policy was still the traditional National Policy of the Conservative party—he promised to use the protective tariff to ensure that Canadian raw materials were manufactured in Canada, thus providing jobs for Canadians. The only thing that Bennett injected that was new was his energy and his conviction. He was the Methodist revivalist, preaching the old gospel but making it sound new and relevant.

"Mackenzie King promises you conference," he said in one campaign speech; "I promise you action. He promises consideration of the problem of unemployment; I promise to end unemployment. Which plan do you like best?" On the tariff, he shouted: "You have been taught to mock at tariffs and applaud free trade. Tell me, when did free trade fight for you? Tell me, when did free trade fight for you? You say our tariffs are only for our manufacturers; I will make them fight for you as well. I will use them to blast a way into the markets that have been closed to you."[3] King promised caution, Bennett promised action. There were enough uneasy or fearful Canadian voters to make Bennett the Prime Minister.

Bennett promised action and he was as good as his word. Six weeks after the election he called a special session of Parliament to deal with unemployment. It was a short session, with only two bills to be discussed. The first bill Bennett described as a palliative. It provided $20 million for relief. Twenty million does not sound like an astronomical sum today but it was a large sum in a total federal budget of less than $500 million. It was also a radical measure because up to that time no federal government had accepted responsibility for supporting the unemployed. The traditional view was that being out of a job was a temporary problem. If a family had no income, the local authorities—the municipalities—were expected to provide relief out of local taxes. This approach was a carry-over from a more self-sufficient rural society. In an industrial community, if a factory closed down, the majority of ratepayers might be affected, and municipal revenues would also decline. The same was true for rural municipalities in western Canada, where a crop failure meant that all farmers in the community needed help. Thus provincial governments had been forced at various times to come to the aid of municipalities. The federal government, however, had not been involved; the need for relief had rarely been so great that it had exceeded the resources of an indivi-

[3] Printed in the Conservative publication, *The Canadian,* June 13, 1930.

dual province. Thus Bennett's $20 million for the winter of 1930 was a major development, and a major extension of the responsibilities of the federal government.

The other measure of the special session was Bennett's remedy for the depression. He increased the tariff on most of the manufactured goods which could be produced in Canada. It was the sharpest tariff increase in Canadian history since John A. Macdonald's tariff changes in 1879. The aim was to give Canadian manufacturers a monopoly of the Canadian market and so enable them to keep their factories open. Bennett estimated that in a short time this would create jobs for some twenty-five thousand unemployed Canadians and that in the long run it would solve the unemployment problem.

These relief grants and higher tariffs were emergency measures. Bennett himself had only the vaguest idea of what they would accomplish. He could not explain, for example, how the $20 million for relief would be spent. Would the federal government pay money directly to the unemployed? Would it spend the money on public works and thus provide jobs? Would it give the money to provincial or municipal governments and let them decide how to spend it? Bennett did not know. He was going to act, he was going to do something, but the details would have to wait. The tariff bill was much the same. There had not been time for a study, industry by industry, to decide which Canadian industries could increase production if foreign competitors were excluded. There was no analysis of markets or costs. It was simpler in an emergency to raise the tariffs and analyse the problem later.

Given the widespread assumption in 1930 that the economic recession was temporary—that it was an emergency situation that would soon disappear—Ben-

nett's measures could easily be justified. He had promised action and he kept his promise. The problem, of
course, was that the temporary recession refused to go
away. If anything, the situation got worse in 1931 and
1932, despite these measures, and even after 1932 there
was no real recovery. Bennett's reaction was the natural response of a man who had already committed himself to a line of action—he argued that his policies had
had some effect; that they had improved the situation
and that the impact of the depression would have been
even worse without them. It was also natural for Bennett to counsel patience for a year or two after the
emergency session. It would take time for the tariff increase to take effect. In the meantime Canadians would
have to wait.

Until 1932, therefore, the Bennett government produced no new or different policies to meet the problems
of the depression. Its expenditures on relief measures
increased. Bennett had talked favourably of public
works as the most productive form of relief expenditures, but the number of Canadians on relief—maybe
two million by 1932—made this impossible. Governments could barely afford to provide food and shelter
for the indigent. To provide the equipment and materials and administration for major construction projects
in addition to these basic needs seemed out of the question. In most cases the direct relief from the federal
government took the form of federal loans or outright
grants to provincial governments, with provincial governments administering the relief programs. Bennett
tried to limit relief expenditures as much as possible;
like most responsible men of his day he believed that
governments should live within their means. If the federal government was to balance its budget its relief
expenditures had to be controlled. In this area, then,
throughout his term of office Bennett continued to be-

have as if relief measures were emergency measures. Federal relief grants were only designed to keep people alive until the crisis was over. In this five-year period, the federal government spent something over $100 million on farm and unemployment relief. It was a large sum but, as Bennett had said in 1930, it was only a palliative. It was not an attempt to end the depression.

The tariff policy was modified in 1932. There were almost no tariff changes after the drastic upward revision of 1930. Further increases were hardly necessary; tariffs were already high enough in most cases to eliminate foreign competition. But a different aspect of the economy did force itself on Bennett's attention. He had begun with the traditional Conservative view of the Canadian economy. His aim, as he explained in 1930, was "to provide that so far as may be possible the requirements of the 10,000,000 people living on the northern half of this continent shall be provided by Canadian producers."[4]

This was logical and straightforward but it tended to overlook the problems of a good many Canadian producers, those for whom the Canadian market was too small and who therefore depended upon export markets. Canadians produced an excess of many natural products: wheat, beef, fish, pulp and paper. Tariffs offered them no advantage. They could compete successfully at home without relying on tariff protection. In the export markets, however, the tariff was, if anything, a disadvantage because other countries were not inclined to admit Canadian products if Canada refused to admit their products in return. By 1932 it was clear that among Canadian producers it was the producers of these natural products and not the manufacturers who were the hardest hit. Manufacturers could pro-

[4]House of Commons *Debates,* September 16, 1930, p. 239.

duce less and so cut expenses by saving on raw materials and wages and at the same time keep a reasonable balance between supply and demand. It was more difficult for farmers or fishermen to affect this balance. An individual farmer could not affect the total world supply of wheat significantly even if he planted no wheat at all. The only way he could increase his income was to produce more wheat and hope he could sell it. This was a vain hope in the 1930s. Foreign countries were restricting their imports and even with widespread crop failures in Canada much of what was grown could not be sold. By 1935 there was an unsold surplus of two hundred million bushels.

Bennett's response to this problem was to look to the Commonwealth for markets for Canada's surplus products. If other Commonwealth countries were prepared to put a high tariff on foreign imports but admit Commonwealth goods at a lower—a preferential—tariff, or even to admit them free, Canadians might be able to sell their surplus products within the Commonwealth. Imperial preference and even imperial free trade were not new ideas in the 1930s. They had been much discussed in Laurier's day. At that time the political implications had received the most attention. That was an era of concern for the future of the Empire, of interest in imperial federation. An Empire trading bloc had seemed to be one way to develop a more united and cohesive Empire. The Conservative party had been the more empire-minded party in those days—at least in political terms. John A. Macdonald's "A British subject I was born, a British subject I will die" had been his reply to a Liberal platform of freer trade with the United States. The talk of an Empire trading bloc had come to nothing; Great Britain had stuck to its traditional policy of free trade (and so no imperial preference) and dominions like Canada had insisted on protecting their manufacturers, even against British competitors. By 1932, however, the situation had changed. Great Britain had finally given up its policy of free trade, and had introduced tariffs on imports. And in Canada, in this emergency, it was natural for Bennett and the Conservative party, with its pro-British traditions, to think in terms of a Commonwealth solution. The result was an Imperial Economic Conference held at Ottawa in the summer of 1932.

The conference can hardly be described as a success. To put it briefly, the representatives from Great Britain and from each dominion wanted to increase exports but were reluctant to increase imports even from other Commonwealth countries. It was not so much a family council trying to resolve a common crisis as a bargaining table with each country trying to drive a hard bargain. Of the delegates, Bennett was undoubtedly the most demanding and the most difficult. For example, he wanted Great Britain to give preferential treatment to Canadian farm products but was not ready to make any significant concessions to British manufacturers in return. He still hoped to protect Canadian industry from outside competition. The first list of concessions he offered proved on inspection to be almost farcical. It became known as the Mickey Mouse list because one of the typical items on which Canada was prepared to reduce its tariff was Mickey Mouse noisemakers! Small wonder that Neville Chamberlain, the Chancellor of the Exchequer, wrote:

Most of our difficulties centred around the personality of Bennett. Full of high Imperial sentiments, he had done little to put them into practice. Instead of guiding the conference in his capacity as Chairman, he has acted merely as the leader of the Canadian delegation. In that capacity he has strained our patience to the limit.[5]

A number of trade agreements were finally negotiated at Ottawa, including one between Great Britain and Canada. Canadian industrialists did not suffer as a result. Some goods which had been imported from the United States would be imported from Great Britain after 1932, but domestic manufacturers were still adequately protected. Canadian farm products were given a tariff preference in the British market. This helped to preserve an export market but it did nothing to bolster the price of farm products. Britain could not absorb all of Canada's surplus production and the prices paid were prices established in world markets.

The Imperial Economic Conference was again followed by a kind of interregnum when Bennett counselled patience. Canadians should not complain. The government, in Bennett's eyes, had done everything that could be done; all that was necessary now was to wait for the trade agreements to take effect.

Many Canadians, however, refused to wait. They demanded that something be done immediately to end the depression, although often they did not have a clear idea of what could or should be done. But Bennett had promised action and they demanded that the federal government take some action, immediately. Bennett's response to these pressures was what one would expect. He was working fourteen hours a day, dedicating himself to the welfare of his country. He had done everything that he considered humanly possible. He felt he had prevented a worse disaster. There was nothing more he could do for the moment. And yet some critics blindly refused to appreciate what he had done.

[5]Diary, August 20, 1932; quoted in K. Feiling, *The Life of Neville Chamberlain* (London, 1946), p. 215.

How could their attitude be explained? To Bennett it was obvious. His critics were either stupid or irresponsible. Their reckless and radical demands were a danger to the precarious balance he had established. In short, his critics were a menace and, if they persisted, he could only conclude that they were unpatriotic and disloyal—attacking the established government of the country. Any government which has no answer for complaints or grievances tends to react this way, to see critics as agitators and demonstrations as civil disobedience. For want of a policy to remedy the situation it falls back on the responsibility of the government to maintain law and order by the use of force.

It was in these years that Bennett gained the reputation of a callous autocrat, the millionaire unmoved by the distress of the poor. He denounced socialists as communists and in one oft-quoted speech advocated crushing these Reds under "the iron heel of capitalism." At times he reacted as if he really believed that the revolution had arrived. In 1932, for example, some three thousand unemployed workers held a convention in Ottawa and asked Bennett to receive a delegation of twelve men. Bennett decided to face the threat of revolution boldly. He would not admit the men into the Parliament Buildings but he would meet the men on the steps outside. He took no chances. That morning an armoured car arrived on Parliament Hill. City policemen paraded up and down Wellington Street in front of the square. Armed detachments of the R.C.M.P. were posted in front of the East and the West blocks; a third detachment, on horseback, was hidden in reserve behind the Centre Block. The men arrived on foot, read their petition, heard a lecture from Bennett about the evils of trying to coerce the government and subvert the constitution, and then, in an anticlimax, quietly left. It seems unreal and incredible. Even a Conservative newspaper protested at the time against what it described as: "the almost craven and un-British things that went on on Parliament Hill yesterday; in this Chicago-like flaunting of fire-arms; in a scene that smacks more of fascism than of Canadian constitutional authority."[6] R.B. Bennett seems actually to have believed that his critics were dangerous revolutionaries.

In spite of the Ottawa Agreements the depression continued and eventually Bennett once more had to act. A new socialist party—the C.C.F.—was established. The Liberal party gained strength; by 1935 the Liberals had won elections in every province except Alberta. In Alberta the Social Credit party under Aberhart emerged from nowhere to win a stunning provincial victory just before the federal election. Even within the Conservative party there was criticism. H.H. Stevens, Minister of Trade and Commerce, had headed a Price Spreads Investigation and had emerged as the champion of the little man and the small retail merchants. Bennett, in his arbitrary way, had first ignored and then criticized Stevens, who thereupon resigned from the government and eventually founded a new opposition party, the Reconstruction party. Behind all this political opposition was the bitterness and disillusionment, rural and urban, with R.B. Bennett as the focus, the scapegoat, the man who was blamed for everything.

Suddenly, in January of 1935, Bennett once more took the offensive. In a series of five radio broadcasts, he talked of major reforms, of a radical transformation of Canadian society. Canadians listening to the speeches were almost dumbfounded to hear the Conservative Prime Minister, the man widely thought of as

[6]Ottawa *Journal*, March 3, 1932.

a reactionary spokesman for Big Business, using the rhetoric of social revolution.

> The old order is gone [he thundered in his first speech]. It will not return.... I am for reform. And, in my mind, reform means Government intervention. It means Government control and regulation. It means the end of *laissez faire.* Reform heralds certain recovery. There can be no permanent recovery without reform. Reform or no reform! I raise that issue squarely. I nail the flag of progress to the mast-head. I summon the power of the State to its support.

Bennett sounded even more radical when he came to the question of relief: "I am against the dole.... The dole is a condemnation, final and complete, of our economic system. If we cannot abolish the dole, we must abolish the system."[7]

Small wonder that Conservatives were startled. Even some Conservative cabinet ministers thought their leader had suddenly become a socialist. Bennett, incidentally, had not troubled to inform them in advance, and they had to listen to the radio like everybody else. Bennett's critics were inclined to be sceptical about this conversion. Their explanation was that there had to be a federal election in 1935 and that Bennett was a demagogue, desperately trying to avoid certain defeat.

The explanation for these New Deal broadcasts is more complex. For one thing, Bennett was not very specific about what he meant by reform. He did refer to unemployment insurance, minimum wages and scaling down mortgages, but these were not new ideas

[7]The broadcasts were printed in a pamphlet entitled "The Premier Speaks to the People," Ottawa, 1935.

in 1935. What was new was that the federal government was now promising to do something. In Canadian terms this meant federal action in areas which the B.N.A. Act had assigned to the provinces. He also referred to anti-combines legislation and, in general terms, to using the government as an instrument of social justice. Again the ideas were current in the 1930s. What was novel was a Conservative prime minister advocating extensive government control and supervision of business. Even this was not socialism. In Bennett's own words: "When capitalism is freed at last from its harmful imperfections, when government exercises the intended measure of regulation over capitalist groups, capitalism will be in fact your servant and not your master." Bennett was trying to preserve, not destroy, the capitalist system.

Why then were the New Deal broadcasts so startling at the time? In part it was because the phrase "The New Deal" was associated with the radical experiments in the United States. Under Roosevelt the early New Deal did attempt to alter the structure of industrial society—it encouraged mergers and cartels on the one hand and trade unions on the other, with the government as a kind of referee. Bennett's New Deal was much less radical, but the label frightened the timid.

There was, however, some connection with the American New Deal. W.D. Herridge, Bennett's brother-in-law, was Canadian Minister to Washington at this time. Herridge realized, as did many New Dealers in the United States by this time, that Roosevelt's New Deal had not been very successful in dealing with the depression. On the other hand it had been successful psychologically—it had convinced many suffering Americans that at least Roosevelt was on their side, and was doing his best for them. One proof of this was the Democratic landslide in the election of 1934. Herridge therefore persuaded Bennett that what was needed in Canada was a psychological New Deal. He argued that much of Bennett's legislation was significant—the Ottawa Agreements, the Central Bank, the Natural Products Marketing Act. The problem was one of public relations, of tying everything together in a dramatic package and so giving the people the feeling that something was happening. As he wrote from Washington in 1934:

> The people still look on [the President] as the man who gave them the New Deal and as a leader who, in some way not wholly revealed, will lead them out of the wilderness of depression.... We [i.e. in Canada] need some means by which the people can be persuaded that they also have a New Deal, and that the New Deal will do everything for them *in fact* which the New Deal here has done *in fancy.*[8]

Bennett, it seems clear, was convinced that he had done a great deal but that Canadians have never realized or understood what he had accomplished. It was easy to believe that dramatic talk of a New Deal would get the message across. With an election imminent, he decided on the radio broadcasts. They may have been even more dramatic than he intended; Herridge came back to Ottawa to help draft them and some of the most striking and colourful phrases were his. In any case, it seems clear that Bennett's New Deal implied some changes—increased centralization in the federal system and increased government intervention in economic affairs—but that it was the packaging which startled Canadians at the time.

[8]R.B. Bennett Papers, W.D. Herridge to R.B. Bennett, April 12, 1934.

Arthur Meighen summed it up well at a federal dinner for Bennett in 1939. Meighen, of course, was an unrevised and unrepentant Conservative who had little sympathy for radical ideas. His comment was, "What a lot of people—timid people—have still in their minds like a nightmare is not the legislation, which was enlightened, but the speeches, which frightened."[9]

The New Deal speeches were broadcast in January of 1935. The rest was almost anti-climax. Bennett's strategy had been to assemble Parliament, allow the Liberal opposition time to attack the government's policies and then to call a snap election. Mackenzie King, however, was too crafty to be caught in this trap. Instead of debating the Speech from the Throne, King refused to express any opinion of the New Deal until the actual legislation was presented. The government was embarrassed, since it had no legislation ready. Hastily drafted bills were introduced one by one. The work of the session almost came to a full stop at one stage because Bennett suffered a mild heart attack. Under normal circumstances he would have resigned. In 1935, however, nothing was normal. One of the leading candidates to succeed him was H.H. Stevens, the minister who had been forced to resign because of a disagreement with his leader. Bennett decided to fight on rather than be succeeded by Stevens. He adjourned the session for six weeks to convalesce in London at an Imperial Conference. By July, when Parliament was dissolved, the broadcasts had become ancient history and the Conservative government campaigned on its record of five years in office.

The result was a devastating repudiation of Bennett's party. Only 39 Conservatives were returned in a House of 245 members; 12 of the 18 cabinet ministers

[9]Toronto *Telegram,* Jan. 17, 1939.

were among the defeated. Bennett himself stayed on until 1938 when a Conservative convention elected R.J. Manion as his successor. A year later Bennett retired to London and eventually entered the House of Lords as Viscount Bennett of Mickleham and of Calgary. He died in 1947, a lonely invalid, ignored and almost forgotten by his compatriots.

It has been said of Richard Bedford Bennett that he destroyed his party while saving his country. Certainly he left the Conservative party shattered. It is less certain that he had saved his country. In financial matters he had been ultra-conservative; his efforts had been directed to retrenchment and balanced budgets. In so doing he had preserved Canada's international credit rating, and of this he was immensely proud. Economists would say, in retrospect, that it would have been better to increase government expenditures but it is hard to criticize a man too severely for not being ahead of his times. A more valid criticism is that Bennett alienated many Canadians, and gave them the feeling that the government was on the side of the more privileged groups in society. In part, it was because of his style, his authoritarian manner, his arrogance and his lashing out at critics. It was no accident that his party was shattered. The fate of his party reflected the increasing disaffection of Canadians with the federal system itself. By failing to give Canadians the feeling that his government was their government, Bennett accentuated the regional and social divisions which are still the dominant factor in the Canada of today. On the credit side of the ledger, he did attract able civil servants to Ottawa and establish some of the institutions of a modern industrial society, such as the Bank of Canada, the C.B.C. and the Wheat Board. The trouble was that these men and these institutions could only operate effectively if Canadians had confidence in them, and R.B. Bennett during his five years in office had lost the confidence of most Canadians in his party and in his government.

Bennett frequently described himself as Chairman of the Board of Directors. He saw himself as the executive, making decisions about the country's business. The shareholders—the citizens of Canada—were expected to trust him or fire him. In 1935 they fired him. Bennett never did realize that there was a difference between business and politics, and that government is more than a question of balance sheets and executive decisions.

5
William Lyon Mackenzie King: The Conciliator in Politics

Mackenzie King is one of the best known and least liked of all our prime ministers. Even today he is a controversial figure; a man who had none of the obvious qualities of a leader and yet a man who survived for an incredibly long time in a very hazardous occupation—he was leader of the Liberal party for almost thirty years and prime minister for over twenty. And not only that, he left an indelible stamp on the country. Whether for good or ill, today's Canada is partly King's making.

Our concern is with the Mackenzie King of the 1930s. Even in those years his contemporaries were puzzled by the man. R.J. Manion, a Conservative opponent, commented that King was unpopular in the House of Commons and among most Canadians. How could such a man win elections? Manion could only suggest that he was an "opportunist, *par excellence*" and also very lucky.[1]

Prominent Liberals were just as ambivalent. J.W. Dafoe of the *Free Press*, for example, was a very partisan critic of R.B. Bennett but he also had reservations about King. Dafoe never sided with the Liberals who wanted to get rid of King—and there were many such Liberals in the early 1930s—but on the other hand he was never prepared to go farther than to say that King, for all his weaknesses, was the best man available. Most party leaders rouse more enthusiasm.

What is the explanation for this ambivalence? The simple answer is that Mackenzie King himself *was* an ambivalent figure. His career is strewn with apparent contradictions and inconsistencies. He seemed to be flabby and indecisive; never yes, never no, always maybe or partly, always the smoke screen of qualifications which concealed any decision, or hid the fact that no decision had been made. And yet this apparently indecisive man picked forceful and powerful colleagues; Gardiner, Dunning, Ralston, C.D. Howe—these men were not nonentities. What is more, King controlled and dominated these men. Ralston he dismissed abruptly, without warning. And C.D. Howe once said that the key to King's career was that King was a leader—a telling remark coming from C.D. Howe! The ambivalence shows up in King's policies too. He posed as a social reformer: the first Minister of Labour, the industrial consultant, the workingman's friend. And yet his record of social legislation is a meagre one, and is as easily explained by political opportunism as by political conviction.

King's political longevity becomes more credible if we begin with his concept of political leadership.

[1]R.J. Manion, *Life is an Adventure* (Toronto, 1937), p. 290.

King did not believe in imposing his will or his policies on his party; he was not an authoritarian leader
like Bennett. King believed that his party, and his
cabinet, had to be consulted and had to be convinced
before a policy could be adopted. He believed in participatory democracy, at least within the party. This
didn't mean that he suppressed his own opinions—
quite often it meant that he converted others to the
policy he preferred. On other occasions, however, it
could mean agreement on a policy or a compromise
for which he had little enthusiasm. Political leadership for him was like being a conciliator in labour
disputes; the successful conciliator is one who comes
to understand the point of view of both sides, and who
can thus suggest a compromise or a settlement which
both sides can accept. The conciliator is not a passive
bystander. He tries to create a satisfactory agreement,
a consensus. He contributes his own ideas as well as
his techniques for arriving at agreement. Although
the final outcome cannot be dictated it is often the result of persuasion.

Mackenzie King's reaction to depression illustrates his activities as a conciliator. Initially King,
like many of his contemporaries, saw the depression
as a temporary recession. It could not be ignored but
at the same time it did not seem to demand drastic or
radical measures. King, in the Liberal tradition, believed at first that the economy would recover with
little help from governments. The important thing,
from his point of view, was not to obstruct the process
but to allow economic laws to operate. Canadian
Liberals saw the protective tariff as the worst form of
obstruction. By creating artificial barriers to trade,
the tariff distorted national economies, and at the
same time taxed the poor for the benefit of the rich. It
was natural therefore for King in the early 1930s to

blame the depression on the tariff which Bennett had just raised to unprecedented levels. Even as late as 1932 King was still focusing on the tariff as the real villain. In the session of that year the Liberal amendment to the budget declared that lower tariffs were "essential to a revival of trade, and improvement of business, and the return of prosperity."

By 1932, however, the traditional emphasis on the tariff no longer satisfied all Liberals. Western Liberals, for example, once so obsessed with the tariff issue, no longer cared. Lower tariffs might reduce the cost of farm machinery but what did this matter when wheat prices were too low to cover the costs of production, much less meet mortgage payments and provide a living? Most westerners by this time had decided that the depression posed new and urgent problems and could only be resolved by new and radical measures. Many of them had come to the radical and almost revolutionary conclusion that the answer lay, not in lower tariffs, but in inflation. Inflation would raise the prices of farm products. It would also raise the prices of the goods which farmers purchased but there would still be a net gain. Most farmers had mortgages on their land and machinery, mortgages based on the inflated prices of the 1920s but which now had to be repaid when dollars were scarce. Inflation, by lowering the value of money, would redress the balance, and make it possible to pay debts in devalued currency. Even in 1932 King had been under strong pressure from western Liberals to go beyond the tariff and opt for some form of inflation. Eastern Liberals were not sympathetic to the idea. They did not represent a debtor community; deliberate inflation was to them shockingly dangerous and even immoral. How could business survive if money had no stable value? There could be no Liberal consensus on inflation under these conditions and so King pacified the westerners by leaving inflation an open question. In the 1932 session at least, the party stayed united on its tariff resolution.

King, however, was sensitive to shifting political currents. Personally he would have been happy to continue to concentrate on the tariff issue; inflation seemed to him morally wrong and unlikely to foster economic recovery. But as party leader he could not ignore the feelings of his western followers. The party must be kept united. If Liberals could not agree to concentrate on the tariff, some new basis of agreement was needed. Inflation did not look like a promising avenue. In addition to King's personal misgivings, it was clear that eastern Liberals would not support that policy.

It was here that King illustrated his capacity for leadership—for his type of leadership. In the fall of 1932 he met with some prominent Liberals, a select group which included Vincent Massey and J.W. Dafoe as well as active politicians like Lapointe and Ralston. They argued about tariff policy, railway policy and, inevitably, about monetary policy. All of these men were Liberals with concern for the underprivileged but also with a healthy respect for free enterprise and existing social institutions. They were not likely to opt for simple panaceas such as printing money. All of them could remember the postwar inflation in Germany a dozen years earlier, when people had gone to the bakery with a wheel-barrow of paper marks for a loaf of bread. But on the other hand, what of the argument that the value of money had already changed during the depression? The depression could be seen as a period of deflation; to say that the prices had declined was only another way of saying that the value of money had increased. Would it be possible to manipulate the money supply to increase prices without having a runaway inflation? How could the money supply be safely adjusted? What about a central bank?

Mackenzie King was intrigued by the possibility. He had once been trained as an economist but he knew little about the complexities of velocity of circulation and rediscount rates, so he consulted Professor Curtis, an economist at Queen's University. From him King learned that a central bank would be necessary if a policy of controlled inflation was ever adopted, but that a central bank did not necessarily mean inflation. Here was the compromise King was looking for. He knew his party could not be united on a policy of inflation but both western and eastern Liberals might be persuaded to agree on the establishment of a central bank. The compromise might be summed up as "inflation if necessary but not necessarily inflation."

It was not enough for King to decide on a policy. Bennett was the kind of leader who announced his decisions in radio broadcasts but for King political leadership involved consultation and discussion. When Parliament reassembled in January of 1933 King therefore announced to caucus that a Liberal platform needed to be hammered out and proposed a number of caucus committees to discuss the various planks. All of the committees—tariffs, railways, social welfare—encountered some difficulty in reaching agreement, but the committee on monetary policy was almost a free-for-all, as he knew it would be. King, however, used all his considerable talent as a conciliator. He attended all the meetings, began by suggesting the central bank as a possible basis of agreement, listened carefully to the contradictory views, drafted what he hoped would be an acceptable policy statement after three weeks, allowed the debate to continue for another two weeks, revised his draft slightly to meet the criticisms and finally got all members of the committee to agree that the draft was at least acceptable—as far as it went. The final consensus was that the Liberal party advocated a central bank. It went farther, however, and also stated that the supply of currency and credit should be determined by the needs of the community.

This was still vague. Liberals might still disagree on what the needs of the community were; but the platform was nonetheless a radical advance in party policy. The Liberal party had affirmed that government should control monetary policy, that it should manipulate currency and credit. Money was no longer sacrosanct; governments on this basis would be as responsible for the supply of money as they were for the level of tariffs or taxes. From King's point of view, what was even more important was that all members of the party had agreed. This policy represented a consensus on which the party was united. It was no mean achievement to have negotiated such a radical shift in policy without alienating any of his followers.

The Liberal platform of 1933 remained the official platform of the party through the election campaign of 1935. It had been difficult enough to arrive at a consensus and King had no urge to open up the Pandora's box and start all over again. In any case, he did not think it was necessary. He was sure that the Liberals would win the next election. It seemed the part of wisdom to be as flexible as possible; to adopt general principles without being committed to specific measures. The party favoured freer trade, closer cooperation with provincial governments, more efficient administration—but few details were spelled out.

It required a good deal of self-confidence to avoid specific promises. Other parties were less reserved.

R.B. Bennett had his New Deal. The C.C.F. had its Regina Manifesto of 1933. H.H. Stevens' Reconstruction party was promising a wide range of measures which would restore prosperity. Social Credit had its inflationary panacea. Many Liberals feared that they would suffer defeat if they did not participate in this auction. King, however, was convinced that the Canadian voters had had enough of reckless and unfulfilled promises. He was sure that they would have more respect for a party which offered a stable and responsible administration. In the welter and confusion of three new parties and a Conservative party which had changed its spots, the Liberal party would offer cautious reform. The Liberal slogan in 1935 was "King or chaos." As a slogan it reflected accurately enough the political situation. The Liberal party was the only party with significant support across the country. If it did not win, there would be no majority government. The slogan also reflected King's view that the Liberal party would win without offering anything more specific. The voters confirmed his analysis: they returned 171 Liberals in a House of 245, the largest majority in Canadian history up to that time.

Any slogan, however, is an oversimplification. Chaos was still possible, even with King in office. The multiplicity of parties in 1935 was a reflection of fundamental divisions within the country. One out of every five voters had voted for new parties, radical parties, parties which had not even existed in 1930. And even within the older parties, Conservative and Liberal, there were differences and divisions which had not been resolved. These political divisions were based on deeply rooted divisions within Canada itself. The grievances of western Canada, for example, explain why both the C.C.F. and Social Credit parties drew their strength from that region. The Liberal party itself was a coalition of regional and cultural blocs, and there was no guarantee that it would hold together in the face of the continuing economic crisis.

Mackenzie King, when he returned to office in 1935, had no new or novel policies. In many ways he was still the King of an earlier era. In 1921 he had come into office during an economic recession. His government had economized, it had balanced its budget and even reduced the national debt, it had lowered tariffs and taxes. Within a few years prosperity had returned, and King believed that there was a cause and effect relationship. He was convinced that these policies had brought prosperity once and that similar policies in the 1930s would produce similar results. He did not close the door on new ideas, but he hoped that the tested remedies of the past would still be effective.

He began with the traditional Liberal policy of freer trade. Within three weeks of taking office he had signed a trade agreement with the United States. Negotiations had begun when Bennett was still Prime Minister but Bennett had not been enthusiastic. King had no reservations, although the implications were far-reaching. It was the first formal trade agreement with the United States since the Reciprocity Agreement of 1854 and it marked the turning away from the ever-increasing tariff barriers between the two countries which had reached their peak with the Hawley-Smoot tariff and the Bennett tariff, both in 1930. A further trade agreement was signed three years later, this time involving Great Britain as well as the United States. The trend was clearly towards increased trade with the United States. It is a trend which has continued ever since until today the relationship is almost symbiotic.

Freer trade, especially with the United States, was expected to benefit Canadian producers of natural

products by increasing their markets. It was a traditional Liberal policy and the effects would be grad-
ual at best. The same traditional and cautious approach could be seen in the first budget of the new
government. No new expenditures were proposed but
corporation taxes and the sales tax were increased.
The aim was to balance the budget, to have the federal
government live within its means.

Even monetary policy scarcely reflected the long-
drawn-out discussion over inflation. R.B. Bennett had
established a central bank in 1934. The Bank of Canada which he set up was a banker's bank, independent
of the federal government and primarily concerned
with financial stability. The Liberal government
amended the constitution of the Bank of Canada to
establish federal control and eventually federal ownership. It was thus in a position to determine the supply
of currency and credit on the basis of the needs of the
community. Under Graham Towers, however, the Bank
of Canada had already established a policy of easy
money. Chartered banks had plenty of money to lend
at low rates of interest. The policy of easy money was
continued but neither Towers nor the government under King was prepared to print more money.

Special measures were introduced for the drought
areas on the prairies, where crop disaster continued to
be almost the normal way of life. Some marginal crop
land was turned back to grazing land and an insurance
scheme was introduced to provide some income for
farmers in a year of crop failure. The Wheat Board,
established under Bennett, was continued under the
Liberal government. What improvement there was,
however—and there was some—had little to do with
federal policies. Crop failures and acreage reductions
in Canada and elsewhere in the world gradually eliminated the world wheat surplus and wheat prices in-

creased, although they were still below a dollar a bushel. The price trend was at least encouraging, and if rains would come and if grasshoppers and rust and frost would stay away, the farmers could hope to get off relief.

At this stage there was nothing radical, nothing really novel, nothing that was not consistent with traditional and orthodox Liberalism. The orthodoxy of the new government is most clearly shown in its efforts to economize, to balance the federal budget. The greatest drain on the budget was still the heavy relief expenditures: unemployment relief and farm relief. Soon after taking office King appointed a National Employment Commission, which was asked to do two things. It was to reorganize the administration of all relief expenditures, in the hope that a more centralized and more efficient administration would eliminate duplication and reduce costs. It was also asked to recommend measures which might be taken to create employment opportunities and so remove men from the relief rolls.

The National Employment Commission was not able to introduce many economies. Most of the relief was administered by provincial and municipal governments and, even though the federal government was providing much of the money, there was little the federal government could do to change the system. It was a different story when it came to recommending positive measures to foster employment. The Commission argued that employment was not a local but a national problem. A factory might close down in Hamilton but the cause was elsewhere—in the declining purchasing power in the Maritimes or the prairies perhaps, where men could no longer afford to buy the products of the factory. Two major conclusions were drawn from this analysis. Because the Canadian economy was national and not local or provincial in scope, unemployment must be seen as a national problem. The Commission therefore recommended that the federal government should take over the full cost of unemployment relief. The Commission went much farther, however; it argued that some positive action could be taken to reduce unemployment. Instead of economizing and trying to balance the budget, it recommended increased federal expenditures and reduced taxation in times of depression. The motor of the economy was seen as investment. When private enterprise was not prepared to invest money—when there was a depression—governments should deliberately incur deficits in order to counterbalance the deficiency. John Maynard Keynes had arrived in Canada.

Mackenzie King's initial response to these suggestions was more than negative: it was hostile. He paid little attention to the positive proposals; he was shocked even at the suggestion that the federal government should pay the full cost of unemployment relief. The federal government was having enough trouble meeting its financial obligations as it was; it seemed absurd to aggravate its problems by taking over more responsibilities. King was reacting like a traditional federalist, insisting that both levels of government, federal and provincial, should look after their own affairs. It was at this time, in the fall of 1937, that King decided to set up yet another royal commission—the Rowell-Sirois Commission on Dominion-Provincial Relations. If the federal system was going to be changed it would not be changed unilaterally, by having the federal government volunteer to take on new burdens.

But the positive proposals of the Employment Commission were not forgotten. The 1938 session might be the last session before the next election. King suggested to the Minister of Finance, Charles Dunning, that he plan a pre-election budget. For King this meant a balanced budget, for he was sure that responsible Canadians wanted a government which lived within its means. Charles Dunning agreed; he too believed that government deficits were undesirable, if not immoral. Dunning's first draft of his budget proposed a small surplus.

King and Dunning, however, were surprised to find that some cabinet ministers no longer believed in balanced budgets. Norman Rogers, Minister of Labour, had been converted by the Employment Commission. He argued that Dunning should budget for a deficit and talked of an additional $40 million for public works to inject money into the economy. Dunning threatened to resign if this policy was adopted; Rogers threatened to resign if it wasn't. Other cabinet ministers took sides. It was the kind of situation in which King the conciliator took over. He was not convinced by the arguments but he was, as always, convinced that the party must be kept united. Eventually he proposed $25 million of additional expenditure as a compromise and set up a cabinet committee to decide how the money would be spent.

The budget of 1938 was a turning point in fiscal policy in Canada. For the first time a government had consciously decided to spend money to counteract a low in the business cycle. In addition to the expenditures in the budget the government also offered loans to municipalities for local improvements and passed a National Housing Act to encourage the building of homes. Consistent with this Keynesian approach, the government also reduced some taxes and offered some tax exemptions for private investors. The idea of a static and balanced budget was gone. In its place was a fiscal policy of stimulating economic recovery by government deficits and by direct economic incentives.

The new fiscal policy did not work any miracles. Recovery would not come until the war, when deficit financing and government investment in the economy became a patriotic duty. But the budget of 1938 marks the beginning of a new concept of the role of government in Canada. Until then the federal government had concentrated on providing public services such as railways and canals, police forces and national defence, post offices, and more recently old age pensions and unemployment relief. The taxes it had collected were designed to pay for these services. It had now undertaken a new and significantly different responsibility: that of balancing the total economic investment, private and public, in order to balance the national economy. The implications would be far-reaching. The government budgets of our day are dominated by this new role. Looking back to the 1930s we can now see that it was the most radical and most constructive innovation of that depression decade.

And yet it is still difficult to visualize Mackenzie King as a radical. He was not an innovator; he was not a man with original ideas. Indeed, he still continued to believe that eventually governments should balance their budgets and let free enterprise flourish. Certainly he did not appreciate the significance of the Keynesian revolution. King's strength was in his commitment to a policy of party unity, and in his capacity to accept and adopt new ideas when the alternative was a division within the party. This concept of political leadership had brought King a long way since 1930. On monetary issues he had begun with the certainty that inflation was sin but had come to accept the idea of a central bank which might manipulate currency and credit on the basis of social need. On fiscal policy he had begun with the traditional ideas of a limited role for government with balanced budgets

and had come to accept the idea of government responsibility for controlling the level of economic activity.

Under King the Liberal party did respond, gradually
and tentatively, to the pressures of a revolutionary
decade, and under his leadership it responded without
disintegrating into warring factions. To be leader of a
still united party four years later was in itself no
small achievement. The risk of party schisms had been
real. More significant, the party still seemed to have
popular support. Mackenzie King's policies had not
been dramatic but his concept of political leadership
had averted possible chaos.

ATLANTIC BAPTIST COLLEGE
MONCTON, N. B.

6
J. S. Woodsworth
– Christian Socialist

Politics is a form of warfare—civilized warfare but still war. Political parties are rival armies, each intent on defeating the enemy, collecting the sinews of war and amassing the battalions for the decisive battle on polling day, with the victor taking over and the vanquished regrouping for the next assault-at-arms, often even dismissing the defeated generals in the hope of finding a more successful leader. The analogy is accepted by politicians—they talk of war-chests, of victory and defeat, and often refer to the opposition as the enemy in their private correspondence. It is all very civilized, of course. The defeated are not imprisoned or executed. Instead they become Her Majesty's Loyal Opposition, where they can criticize the government and continue to manoeuvre but nonetheless are effectively excluded from the seats of the mighty.

J. S. Woodsworth was an unusual participant in political war games. He had been a Methodist minister, and even after he became a politician he was described by his biographer as a "prophet in politics." It was also unusual that leaders of other parties maintained a certain respect for Woodsworth even though he was an opponent. Here for example is a statement by Mackenzie King, a public statement in the House of Commons, and moreover, one that was made at the outbreak of war in 1939. Woodsworth was a pacifist and was against Canadian participation. Yet King took this opportunity to praise Woodsworth.

> There are few men in this Parliament for whom, in some particulars, I have greater respect than the leader of the Co-operative Commonwealth Federation. I admire him in my heart because time and again he has had the courage to say what lay on his conscience regardless of what the world might think of him. A man of that calibre is an ornament to any Parliament.[1]

It would be wrong, however, to write off J. S. Woodsworth as a mere ornament. He was a saintly man, a prophet crying in the wilderness, a man of conscience judging events by the test of Christian morality. But he also went to jail for his part in the Winnipeg strike. He was the founder of a political party and he dominated it in its formative years. He was not a successful politician, in the sense of leading his party to victory, but he was at least indirectly responsible for some of the social welfare legislation between the wars. He was, in Frank Underhill's phrase, "an untypical Canadian."

Our concern is with the career of J. S. Woodsworth during the 1930s. How was it that in this decade

[1]House of Commons *Debates,* September 8, 1939, p. 19.

Woodsworth became the leader of a new party, a socialist party? And what form did his socialism take in Canada during the depression? What groups in Canadian society turned to this new party in those years? What answers did the C.C.F. offer for the depression? And finally, why did Woodsworth resign as leader of the party at the end of the decade? The answers to these questions are essential to any discussion of Woodsworth's career. They are also important for any discussion of Canadian society during the depression.

The activities of J. S. Woodsworth in the 1930s can only be understood if we begin with his earlier life and see how he became involved in politics in the first place. Woodsworth was the son of a Methodist minister who moved from Ontario to Manitoba in the early days of settlement. He himself went into the ministry and took up his first charge in 1900. But Woodsworth, as a young man, reflected a new strain in the religious faith of that day. For him the gospel was the social gospel— the belief that Christians should work for a Christian society here on earth rather than in the hereafter. Woodsworth as a student did settlement work in the slums of London. A few years after his ordination he went to the All People's Mission in North Winnipeg, where he worked with new immigrants and with the displaced and rejected who congregate in urban slums.

The social gospel went far beyond preaching the word of God from the pulpit. It also went far beyond administering charity to the unfortunate. Instead of individual salvation it put the emphasis on the social environment. Drunkenness and prostitution were immoral but could individuals be blamed for these sins if they lived in squalor, uneducated, with no prospect of improving their lot, where even to survive meant no more than continuing a purposeless existence? And what of the children in communities where parents had no ambition and no hope, children who lived in tenements and never went to school? The social gospel wanted the Kingdom of God on earth. Prayer was not enough. Charity, love and brotherhood meant that everyone was responsible for his neighbour. Working with the poor quickly convinced men like Woodsworth that these people could not be expected to lead responsible Christian lives until they escaped from the pressing problems of poverty. Men could lead only an animal existence if they faced a daily struggle to find food and shelter.

J. S. Woodsworth was a sensitive and also a very dedicated Christian. His commitment to the social outcasts of North Winnipeg led him gradually but inevitably into politics. He raised questions about an immigration policy which brought so many who could not adjust to pioneer life. When his suggestions for more careful selection of immigrants and more help for them in adjusting after their arrival fell on deaf ears, Woodsworth came to the conclusion that many Canadians wanted it that way, that they looked on immigrants as a commodity, as cheap labour. The cure was not to be found in North Winnipeg but with businessmen and politicians who were really responsible for creating North Winnipeg. Thus the blame for living conditions in a slum rested, not with the poor, but with the rich and powerful who tolerated and in some cases benefited from them. Here for example is a letter which Woodsworth wrote to the *Manitoba Free Press* in 1909.

Some of these people may be lazy and shiftless. Small wonder when they are forced into conditions which foster idleness, immorality and crime. And behind all, the fact remains that there is not work for them. Let me tell you of one little foreign girl. She lives in a room in a disreputable old tenement

—one of those human warrens which are multiply-
ing with great rapidity in our city. Her father has
no work. The men boarders have no work. The
place is incredibly filthy. The little girl has been
ill for months—all that time living on the bed in
which three or four persons must sleep and which
also serves the purpose of table and chairs. For
weeks this little girl has had itch which has spread
to the children of the surrounding rooms. She has
torn the flesh on her arms and legs into great sores
which have become poisoned. The other day I saw
the mother dip a horrible dish rag into the potato
dish and wash the sores! I took a friend to see the
child. The mother started to show us the child's
arm. The dirty dress was stuck in the great open
sores. As the scabs were pulled away from the
quivering flesh the little one writhed and screamed
in agony. My friend who has dear little girlies of
his own, half gasped, half cried, "My God! This is
damnable!" As we stumbled down the stairs I heard
him muttering between clenched teeth, "God, to
think of my Isabelle in a place like that!" The little one still lives there in her misery. Is there not
some man or some woman who has a heart and a
head who will help that child? . . . Yes, and many of
the well-to-do are drawing large revenues from this
same misery. A few months ago it was openly
stated before the police Commission that the
owners of some of the vilest dens in the city were
our "best" (!) people—our society people, our church
people, and that for these houses they obtain in
some cases, double the legitimate rentals.[2]

The shift from welfare work to political action was

[2]*Manitoba Free Press*, March 12, 1909, quoted in K. Mc-
Naught, *A Prophet in Politics* (Toronto, 1959), pp. 56-57.
This account of Woodsworth's formative years is heavily
indebted to Professor McNaught's biography.

accelerated by the war. Woodsworth believed that wars solved nothing, and that they distracted attention from the problems which seemed to him to be important. His experiences at this time completed his disillusionment with the leaders of Canadian society. A quotation from a letter to his wife, written during a visit to Montreal in 1915, shows how even the church seemed to him to be acting as an agent of the state.

> In the evening I went to St. James' Methodist Church to a recruiting meeting. Really, Lucy, if I wasn't on principle opposed to spectacular methods I would have gotten up and denounced the whole performance as a perversion—a damnable perversion if you like—of the teachings of Jesus and a profanation of the day and the hour set aside for Divine worship. War exhortations favour the Hebrew prophets. It was significant that there was no New Testament lesson. War anthems and hymns with war phrases sung as war hymns, the national airs of the allied nations rendered by the organ ...
>
> A deliberate attempt was made through a recital of the abominable acts of the Germans to stir up the spirit of hatred and retaliation. The climax was reached when the pastor in an impassioned appeal stated that if any young man could go and did not go he was neither a Christian nor a patriot. No! the climax was the announcement that recruiting sergeants were stationed at the doors of the church and that any man of spirit—any lover of his country—any follower of Jesus—should make his decision then and there.[3]

You could preach patriotism from the pulpit but there was no place for Woodsworth's version of Christian

[3]J. S. Woodsworth to his wife, November 26, 1915; quoted in K. McNaught, *op. cit.*, p. 70.

responsibility. He resigned from the ministry, lost his job as secretary of the Canadian Welfare League and for a short time actually worked as a stevedore on the Vancouver docks.

The shift to active politics really came in 1919 with the Winnipeg General Strike. The strike is a fascinating story in itself but here we can only deal with its influence on Woodsworth's career. Woodsworth returned to Winnipeg after the strike had begun. He became directly involved when the editors of the strikers' newspaper were arrested. He took over as editor and in his turn was arrested for "seditious libel." Sedition is a serious offence. Woodsworth's crime was that he had quoted the prophet Isaiah who, two thousand years earlier, had denounced the rich and powerful for exploiting the poor. It was pointed out at the time that if Isaiah had still been alive he too would have been arrested. It must be remembered that there was a widespread fear of revolution in Canada in 1919. The communist revolution in Russia was a frightening example of what could happen if the workers seized power. In the end Woodsworth was never brought to trial; the charges were dropped nine months later. Woodsworth's part in the strike, however, won him the confidence of workingmen. In 1921 he was elected as a labour M.P. from a working-class district in Winnipeg.

By this time Woodsworth's political philosophy had taken shape. For him the shift from the Christian ministry to socialism had not been a radical change. He still saw his life as a life of service, working to bring the Kingdom of God on earth. His concern was still for the underprivileged and the neglected. Christian charity for him was focused on social justice. What had changed was Woodsworth's analysis of the causes of poverty and injustice. Slums and drunkenness and broken families were only symptoms of a deep-rooted social malaise. Such conditions existed because men in authority worshipped Mammon rather than God, and were more concerned with making money than loving their neighbour. But it was more than the individuals; it was the system. Business, politics, even the organized churches, had been shaped by the system and perpetuated it. The only way to reform Canadian society was to eradicate capitalism. The aim was to replace the profit motive by the motive of Christian charity. It sounded simple, but it would mean a radical transformation of every institution in Canada, as well as a radical change in the attitudes of most Canadians.

Woodsworth's analysis of the ills of Canadian society meant that for him the depression of the 1930s came as no surprise. He was already familiar with the depression; there had always been a depression in North Winnipeg. Now the contagion had spread but it was the same disease and required the same remedy. The real difference was that in the 1920s Woodsworth had been a voice crying in the wilderness. After 1930 more and more people agreed that it was not the fault of individuals if they were poor and unemployed. If it wasn't the fault of individuals it must be the fault of the system. Suddenly Woodsworth's message seemed relevant; it seemed to explain why there was a depression, and to hold out hope for ending it.

By 1930, however, J. S. Woodsworth was more than just a man with a message. He had formed close personal contacts with three groups: labour leaders, radical farm leaders in western Canada, and socialist intellectuals in Canadian universities. Woodsworth had been elected as a labour candidate and throughout the 1920s he had been a spokesman for labour. His contact with farm leaders was more fortuitous. The moderate Progressives had been lured back into the Liberal fold by Mackenzie King. The more radical Progressives, however, had maintained their identity as a separate group in the Opposition. It was natural for Woodsworth and these Progressives to cooperate in the House of Commons; more and more they found that they shared similar views. Woodsworth, for example, was opposed to massive immigration because of his experience in Winnipeg; the radical Progressives came to the conclusion that immigration was also a hazard for prairie farmers because more farmers meant over-production and falling prices for farm products. With the depression the Progressives turned to a more radical criticism of the existing system. They saw inflation as the only remedy for farmers who received little for what they produced and had mortgages and other debts to pay off. Woodsworth had long been advocating state control of money and credit instead of leaving it to capitalists. Woodsworth became the leading figure in this parliamentary group; with the depression his pre-eminence was even more clearly established. Outside of Parliament, Woodsworth had also built up contacts with left-wing university professors: such men as Frank Underhill of Toronto and Frank Scott of McGill. These men, like Woodsworth, were critics of the capitalist system. They corresponded and discussed social problems with Woodsworth and looked to him as the one member of Parliament who spoke their language.

All of this suggests that Woodsworth was a very unusual person. It is a rare individual who is at ease in the company of workers, of farmers and of intellectuals and who has the respect of each of these three very different groups. The C.C.F. party was a socialist party with a difference because of Woodsworth's broad contacts and prestige.

The Co-operative Commonwealth Federation was

officially founded and baptised at Regina in July of 1933. Its platform—the Regina Manifesto—bore the stamp of the intellectual who drafted the original version. It spoke of a new social order, of replacing the capitalist system by economic planning, of replacing the profit motive by democratic control of natural resources and the means of production, of using political power to establish economic equality and social justice. The details of the platform—including amendments introduced at the Regina convention—show the labour and farmer influences. There was a labour code, with collective bargaining, unemployment insurance and social insurance for Canadian workers. There was to be state control of currency and credit, with the implication of inflation, for the Canadian farmers.

A political alliance of workers and farmers, however, is not easy to cement. Their interests are not identical and may even be contradictory. Workers are concerned with higher wages and better working conditions, both of which raise the cost of goods which farmers buy. Farmers on the other hand want higher prices for their products, which means higher prices for the food that workers must buy. Only the crisis of a depression could unite these two groups to make common cause. Desperation makes strange bedfellows.

Even so the Regina Manifesto was a compromise. Government ownership of the means of production is a dogma of socialism but when applied to farming it means state ownership of land. This explains why farmers are not usually socialists. The Regina Manifesto, however, made an exception in the case of farm land. It said nothing about nationalizing farms. Instead it guaranteed security of tenure for farmers; in effect promising to protect them against mortgage foreclosures. The C.C.F. was a socialist party but it was not a doctrinaire party.

Labour and farmer support for the C.C.F. cannot be explained fully by desperation and by compromises. There was also J. S. Woodsworth, the unanimous choice for leader and the man who had the confidence of both workers and farmers. Many were sceptical about whether this hybrid party could survive. J. W. Dafoe commented at the time that it was really a labour party with farmers already uneasy with their new associates. In 1933 and for many years to come Woodsworth was the key figure in the socialist party, the man who kept it together and strengthened the uneasy union. Probably more important, Woodsworth made the C.C.F. respectable. It was not easy to make socialism respectable in the Canada of the 1930s. Any critics of the capitalist system were promptly identified as communists and revolutionaries—dupes of Soviet Russia, plotting against king and country and motherhood and everything else that was sacred. J. S. Woodsworth made it more difficult to make this image seem real. This gentle, kindly Christian man with his message of charity and brotherhood was not the stuff of which revolutionaries, anarchists and assassins were made.

Woodsworth also did more than reassure people by his character. The C.C.F. faced a problem common to most left-wing political parties of the time. This was the era of the popular front, when the communist line was to cooperate with social democrats in a common front against fascism. The Communist party in Canada was small but it was vocal and active. Some C.C.F.-ers, usually from labour, were prepared to cooperate. Farmers, especially Ontario farmers, were ill at ease with organized labour from the beginning and the thought of cooperating with communists was anathema. As early as 1934 the United Farmers of Ontario officially withdrew its affiliation with the C.C.F. as a result. Woodsworth was not able to prevent this schism but he did take prompt action against any alliance with the Communist party. One section of the Ontario C.C.F. was actually expelled because it was pro-communist. Woodsworth was a gentle man but he was also a man of rigid principles. Under his leadership the C.C.F. gradually established its identity as a democratic socialist party, distinct and distinguishable from communism.

In the election of 1935 the C.C.F. nominated over one hundred candidates. The total vote for the C.C.F. was just under 400,000. This was less than 10 per cent of the total popular vote but it was nonetheless a sizeable vote for a new and radical socialist party. It was obvious, however, that the party was not yet a national party. There were no C.C.F. candidates in the Maritimes and only three in Quebec—and these three were from urban ridings with a large English-speaking population. The regionalism of the C.C.F. became even more obvious after the election. Of the 7 C.C.F. members elected, there were two from Manitoba, two from Saskatchewan and three from British Columbia. (There were none from Alberta because there the Social Credit swept everything before it.) The C.C.F. had garnered votes in Ontario but not enough in any single constituency to elect a candidate. It was significant that no French Canadian of any influence had joined the party, and that Maritimers had shown little interest. Even west of the Ottawa River it was not certain that the C.C.F. voters were converts to socialism. The success in the western provinces (as well as the success of Social Credit in Alberta) suggested that it was a protest vote—the reaction of men crushed by the depression, frustrated by the inactivity of the older parties, and desperately turning to any party which seemed to offer an alternative to the domination of eastern industrial and financial interests. It was still possible, and even probable, that the C.C.F. would prove to be a temporary aberration, a product of the depression which would disappear if prosperity returned.

In the years from 1935 to the end of the decade, Woodsworth and his followers continued to preach the gospel of socialism. By this time, however, a new factor had emerged. Until this time, the C.C.F. had concentrated on domestic problems, on the plight of the poor and the underprivileged in Canada. British socialists, and especially the Fabians, had largely provided the socialist theories and arguments which the C.C.F. applied within a Canadian context. From 1935 on, however, Canada's relations with the outside world could not be ignored. Manchuria, Ethiopia, the Spanish Civil War, Austria, Czechoslovakia and Munich: the long series of international crises reminded all Canadians that they lived in a carnivorous world.

International affairs have always complicated life for socialists. Karl Marx's analysis of the class struggle led logically to the conclusion that socialists should be against wars. Capitalism led inevitably to international rivalry for raw materials and markets. In this context, wars were only a more intensified form of this competition between the governing classes of different countries. Why should workers serve as cannon fodder and fight each other in such a war when the real enemy for them was the capitalist system? Most socialists, including socialist theoreticians in the C.C.F., agreed with Marx that wars were capitalist wars, with their roots in economic rivalries and economic imperialism. Why should ordinary men sacrifice their lives in these struggles?

This attitude was strengthened by the widespread anti-war sentiment in North America in the 1930s. The First World War was still a horrible example of what war meant, and subsequent events in Europe suggested that the war, for all its sacrifices, had settled nothing. In the United States many believed that American participation in the war had been a dreadful blunder and they were determined that it should never happen again. This attitude lay behind the Senate Committee under Senator Nye, which blamed American involvement on the munitions industry that had profited from the war, and led to the neutrality legislation which prohibited any future sale of munitions manufactured in the United States to any nation at war.

Canadians shared the same isolationist sentiments. J.S. Woodsworth, himself a pacifist, was convinced that no war could be justified. For the C.C.F. there was the added objection that if Canada did get involved in a European struggle again, the concentration on the war effort, and the tremendous expenditures involved, would prevent social reforms at home. Thus for many reasons the C.C.F. was isolationist. In 1936 its National Council passed a resolution in favour of Canadian neutrality in the event of any war. In 1937 this was amended to read "any imperialist war," but the amendment changed little, since to socialists almost every war was by definition an imperialist war.

The C.C.F., however, could not be truly neutral, whatever their theory might be. In the Spanish Civil War, for example, their sympathies were clearly with the Loyalists against Franco. Nor could they be neutral when Germany and Italy and Japan were seen not only as aggressive imperialist powers but also as fascist powers, dedicated to crushing all forms of socialism in Europe.

The test came when war broke out in 1939. Woodsworth favoured neutrality for Canada. He still believed that it was a war between capitalist, imperialist forces. Many other members of the C.C.F. National Council disagreed. They saw it as a war between fascism and democracy. Some of them were also unconsciously influenced by patriotism, by loyalty to king and empire. The Council was divided. Eventually a compromise was proposed; the C.C.F. would support the war effort to the extent of supplying food and munitions to Britain and France but would oppose sending troops. The majority on the Council voted for this compromise. Woodsworth voted with the minority.

It was a tragic end to Woodsworth's career. The socialist party which he more than any other man had brought into existence had forsaken what was for him a fundamental principle. There was no personal animosity; Woodsworth was too charitable and his followers admired him too much for that. He resigned as leader of the party but was named Honorary President. He never recovered from the crisis, however. Eight months later he suffered a stroke and in 1942 he died.

The C.C.F. party survived the crisis. J. S. Woodsworth had managed to weld workers, farmers and intellectuals into a socialist party and to develop a sense of common purpose which survived his death. His dedication to the underprivileged and to the socialist movement remained a basic tradition of the C.C.F. The party was and continued to be a minority party, but a party which exerted an influence that could not be measured by statistics. Woodsworth was, in his daughter's phrase, "a man to remember."

7

Maurice Duplessis
and la survivance

The province of Quebec is not a province like the others. This has become painfully obvious now that confrontation between Quebec and Ottawa has become almost the pattern of Canadian politics, and when some French Canadians have become convinced that Quebec is so different and so unique that the most logical step is for Quebec to become a separate and independent state. But Quebec has never been a province like the others. It did not escape the depression in the 1930s; there were soup kitchens and relief vouchers in the cities and shrivelling incomes on the farms just as there were in other parts of Canada. The depression, however, had a different impact in Quebec because Quebec was different. French-Canadian society had a different structure and different values, and so the French-Canadian reaction to the economic crisis was not the same.

The rest of Canada paid very little attention to what was going on in Quebec in those years. English-speaking Canadians had problems of their own, and Quebec was largely ignored. There was a general belief that French Canada was backward and reactionary; it was thought of as a Roman Catholic province—a priest-ridden province, to use a recurring phrase of the period. It was also vaguely realized that some French-Canadian intellectuals, such as Abbé Groulx, were critical of the federal union, and had some vision of a Laurentia, an independent French state in North America. But intellectuals are always having utopian visions and cannot expect to be taken seriously. There were reports of a fascist movement in Quebec—Adrien Arcand's blueshirts—as well as a good deal of publicity for Maurice Duplessis's notorious Padlock Law. But to most Canadians outside of the province of Quebec, none of this seemed really important. Quebec seemed remote and harmless. Why should English Canadians worry about a province which, for all its apparent faults, was a kind of ghetto, turned in on itself and not really causing much trouble? Nothing ever changed in the province of Quebec, and nothing ever would really change. Or so it seemed. And so English Canadians ignored French Canada, little realizing that the events in Quebec in the 1930s were important and that the issue of cultural duality would eventually become the dominant issue in Canadian politics.

In every part of Canada during the depression, however, the story begins with poverty and privation. In the rural areas of Quebec, as elsewhere, family incomes almost disappeared as the prices of farm produce plummeted. Farmers in Quebec had never been very prosperous; much of the land was sub-marginal and offered only a meagre living at the best of times. French-Canadian leaders in the past had encouraged settlement on the rock-strewn soil of the Gaspé and northern Quebec. They had seen this as a way of preserving the identity of French-Canadian society. Only in the rural parish, it was believed, could French Canadians remain French-speaking and Roman Catholic, and maintain the integrity of the family and the traditional virtues of rural life.

French Canadians were not unique in extolling the rural virtues. Many people idealized life on the farm, far from the madding crowd and the hectic pressures and vices of urban life. The French Canadians, however, carried this view to extremes. For them there were no shadings of grey between the morality of the country and the depravity of the city. A French-Canadian intellectual summed up this attitude in a speech he delivered in 1933.

> Every country, one might say, is governed by this law. The land is the real wealth of nations. It furnishes the men; it sustains them.... The provider for our physical life, the land is also the protector of our moral life. Nature is close to God. It links the soul to the Creator, whose presence can always be felt.... Thus the rural population is always healthier, simpler and more faithful than urban populations. Happy the country where rural society dominates.... A strong race of farmers rooted to the soil: there is our salvation.

The speaker contrasted this healthy and virtuous life with the shocking misery and corruption of the city:

> The atmosphere in which the city-dwellers live is constantly polluted by the fetid odours and harmful smog of factories.... The houses are scarcely any better. Often built without any concern for hygiene, to lodge as many people as possible, they

offer niggardly amounts of the air and light so
necessary for good health. Add to all this, the
noise, the dangerous promiscuity, the depressing
working conditions. How, in such a milieu, can
human lives blossom, expand and develop?[1]

So much for oratorical platitudes. They played their
part in Quebec in attracting and keeping some French
Canadians on sub-marginal lands. Life on the farm,
however, bore little similarity to this vision of the
healthy peasant, God's partner in the noble work of
tilling the soil. Jean-Paul Desbiens was two years old
when the depression began. His father was a *bucheron*,
a woodsman who worked in the *chantiers* in winter
when there was work. Desbiens's recollections are of
poverty, of the almost total absence of money:

At school [he recounts] I learned to type. My
father was in the *chantiers*. I thought it would be
smart, to show him how I was progressing by typ-
ing him a letter. He told us later how dreadfully
upsetting this letter was....He could not read...
He got the letter one morning just before leaving
for the woods. There was no one there to read him
the letter. He had to wait until that evening. And
all day he assumed that it was a letter from a lawyer, since it was typed. And a letter from a lawyer,
that meant a demand for payment with the threat
of legal seizure. In any case, seizure or not, it would
be necessary to pay the lawyer's fees. A lawyer's
letter was, in itself, a catastrophe.[2]

As Desbiens comments, a simple story like that says
a great deal.

[1] J. P. Archambault, S. J., in Semaine Sociale du Canada,
XIIe session, Rimouski, 1933, p. 20. (Translated)
[2] Jean-Paul Desbiens, *Sous le soleil de la pitié* (Montréal,
1965), p. 18. (Translated)

But what of life in the city? For it must be remembered that, in spite of all the platitudes and all the propaganda about rural life, Quebec was an industrialized, urbanized province by the 1930s. More than half the population lived in towns or cities, and Montreal was the largest metropolis in Canada. In Quebec also there was unemployment and the dole in the cities, but there as elsewhere men and families were migrating from farms to cities, looking for work, crowding already bursting tenements or building shoddy shacks on the outskirts of the town. In a sociological study of Drummondville, a small industrial city, Everett Hughes describes a new working-class suburb:

There all is new, all is cheap and barren, all is French. The most consistent and definitive physical phenomenon of the growth of this town is precisely this satellite of some 6,000 souls, housed in cheap barracks and shanties saved from utter shabbiness only by their newness. The imposing church and presbytery rise from the sand lots in a bare angularity which the few small planted trees have not yet softened....Beyond the industries, spreading over the sandy plain, are the clusters of cubical wooden boxes, urban in form but rural in appointments, which house the masses of industrial workers.[3]

But Hughes found more than the beginnings of an industrial slum in Drummondville. For him, the most remarkable feature was the survival of rural attitudes, rural customs and a rural way of life among these industrial workers. On the fringes of the town were the

[3] E. C. Hughes, *French Canada in Transition* (Chicago, 1943), p. 39.

box-shaped frame houses of rural Quebec, and also "ramshackle tenements whose squalor still reeks more of the barnyard than of the city slum."[4] French-Canadian society, with its commitment to the ideal of the rural parish and with its suspicion of urban vicious-ness, had not prevented this migration to the cities but it had done little to prepare the newcomers for city life. Most French-Canadian leaders still turned their backs on urban problems in the 1930s. They almost ignored the plight of French Canadians in the cities because, for them, the future of French Canada was still in the rural parish. When they talked of ending unemployment, they thought of opening up still more land in northern Quebec, of putting these men back on the farm. When they talked of industry, they thought of local crafts for farmers' wives and children to sup-plement farm income.

There was one exception, the exception which proved the rule. Camillien Houde was for a few years the spokesman of the urban proletariat in Montreal. Houde was a short, stout man with little education but with tremendous energy, who spoke the working-class vernacular and whose demagogic attacks on the rich and on the Establishment crystallized the frustrations of the city workers. Houde, unfortunately, had little to offer except words. Some said he was bought off by the industrialists of Montreal; others said it was by the Liberal party. In any case, Houde never used his popular support to achieve social reforms. He could get himself elected mayor of Montreal but he had no policy, no program and no sense of direction. Nor did he have any support among the French-Canadian elite. He represented the grievances of a large group but it

[4] *Ibid.*, p. 38.

was a group which was still considered to be on the fringe of French-Canadian society.

Everett Hughes, in his study of Drummondville, highlighted another characteristic of industrial Quebec —the existence of an English-speaking upper class: the industrialists, the factory managers, the engineers, the accountants, the superintendents. In a city in which the population in 1931 was 91 per cent French-speaking, the largest textile mill in Drummondville employed only one French Canadian above the rank of foreman—and he was the company doctor—although more than twenty-three hundred of the employees of the mill were French Canadians. Nor was Drummondville an exceptional case. In Montreal the banks, the financial institutions, the large corporations, were nearly all owned and managed by English-speaking people; the filing clerks and secretaries were French. Walking down St. James Street one would hardly know that the majority of the citizens of Montreal were French-speaking; certainly no one would think of saying that they were on la rue St. Jacques!

It would be hard to exaggerate the importance of the fact that in Quebec the rich were usually English-speaking and the poor were usually French-speaking. Industrialization is always accompanied by conflicts between capital and labour; in Quebec, however, capital was English and labour was French. What would have been a labour dispute elsewhere was often complicated in Quebec because it was also a dispute between English and French. Grievances against an employer became grievances against *les Anglais*. Almost every crisis in Quebec eventually becomes dominated by the issue of English-French relations.

The depression of the 1930s was no exception. The problems of rural Quebec, of the rural parish and *la survivance*, which at first seemed so peculiarly and so narrowly a French-Canadian problem, could not be isolated from the problems of the English-language corporations. The industrial problem of unemployment, at first glance an economic problem, was also almost inevitably transformed into a cultural problem. And out of it all came, not a radical, socialist or left-wing movement for reform, but a nationalist movement; a French-Canadian, rather than a farmers' or workers' movement, a French-Canadian movement which used the rhetoric of ethnicity and race rather than the rhetoric of occupation or class. The problems of the depression, rural and urban, were translated into problems of French versus English, with the result that little was done to resolve the economic problems of the depression. It so happened that not much was done to deal with the problem of French-English relations either—but this was the problem on which most of the attention was focused.

As everywhere in the 1930s, the struggle took place in the political arena. At the provincial level the decade began with the Liberals in office, as they had been since 1897. Alexandre Taschereau was the Premier, and the Conservative opposition was scarcely visible. By mid-decade, the Liberal party had been shattered, and rebellious young Liberals had allied themselves with Conservatives to form the Union Nationale. The story of how this new political party was formed and came to power is central to the story of Quebec during the depression. The story of Quebec's relations with the federal government, first under Taschereau and then under Duplessis, is another facet of this study.

Louis-Alexandre Taschereau was a member of one of the most prominent Quebec families. His uncle had been a cardinal, his brother was Chief Justice of the

Supreme Court, and Taschereau himself was a member of the provincial Assembly for over thirty years and Premier of the province for sixteen. Not surprisingly, his policies were orthodox and traditional. He accepted without question the importance of rural Quebec as the bastion of French-Canadian society and even in the 1920s his government took pride in its work of opening up new settlements and building roads and schools in rural areas. It is not irrelevant to note that the distribution of seats in the province favoured rural areas. The Montreal region, with a quarter of the population, only elected one-tenth of the members of the Assembly. This is a further illustration of the prestige of rural society in the province.

Nonetheless, Taschereau also had close connections with financial and industrial interests. This was less paradoxical than it seems. There was no obvious conflict between the interests of rural Quebec and of big business. The factories and financial institutions located in the cities had little direct contact with the farming population. As for the paper mills and mines in northern Quebec, they complemented the rural communities there. This was poor farming land and rural families would not have survived if farmers and their sons had not been able to supplement their income by working in the woods—in the *chantiers*—through the winter. By encouraging the establishment of new paper mills the Taschereau government was also encouraging the establishment of new settlements. The Liberal party also benefited because the corporations made large financial contributions to the party in exchange for the concessions which they received from the government. All in all it appeared to be a very harmonious collaboration between English-speaking capitalists and French-speaking rural Quebec, and a very cozy system for a Liberal party financed by the capitalists and elected by the rural vote. It was a system which paid little attention to urban problems or the rights of wage-earners, but it was a system which helped to keep the Liberals in office for forty years.

The Taschereau system also led logically, in federal affairs, to the championing of provincial rights. In the 1920s the federal government under Mackenzie King and Lapointe was becoming interested in the problems of an industrial society. The Liberal platform of 1919 had included the traditional Liberal statement favouring tariff reductions but it had also included a special section on labour and industry, advocating the right of collective bargaining, an eight-hour day, unemployment insurance, sickness insurance and old age pensions. This labour and welfare legislation would require constitutional amendment because under the B.N.A. Act such legislation came under provincial jurisdiction. Taschereau, associated as he was with financiers and industrialists, was inevitably opposed to the federal policies, and he adamantly refused to consider any amendments to the B.N.A. Act which would allow the federal government to implement them.

His reaction to old age pensions illustrates his attitude. In 1927 the federal government circumvented the constitution by passing an Old Age Pensions Act. The federal government would pay half the cost of the pensions but the act would only come into effect in those provinces which passed enacting legislation and agreed to pay the other half. Taschereau refused to participate, and Quebec did not join until 1936, by which time the federal government had increased its portion to three-quarters of the total cost and the Liberal party in Quebec was desperately trying to stave off defeat by the Union Nationale.

There were many reasons for the difficulties in which the provincial Liberal party found itself by the mid-1930s. Any party in office for almost forty years has problems; it is never easy for a government to realize that policies which have been popular in the past may no longer be sufficient. In the 1930s many young Liberals were frustrated because the old guard made all the decisions; they were even more frustrated because they wanted new measures to meet the problems of the depression. The Action Libérale Nationale, as these young dissidents called themselves, was at first intended to be a reform movement within the Liberal party. The problem was that the Liberal party under Taschereau refused to be reformed.

The Action Libérale Nationale was not that radical. The first plank in its platform asserted "that economic recovery is mainly the task of restoring rural prosperity, based on the family farm and cooperation. This is why we give agricultural reforms the highest priority in our plan of action."[5] There were subsequent references to the rights of labour but these were traditional rights: accident insurance, maximum hours, minimum wages and the like. Significantly it did not refer to trade unions or the right of collective bargaining. The A.L.N. was clearly not a socialist party.

These dissident Liberals did differ from Taschereau in their attitude toward big corporations. Instead of believing that big business was of benefit to rural Quebec they were convinced that corporations were exploiting the poor. The A.L.N. was especially bitter against the pulp and paper industry and the hydro-electric power companies, which it believed were callous cartels, interested only in shareholders' profits.

[5]The full text is printed as an Appendix in H.F. Quinn, *The Union Nationale* (Toronto, 1963).

This still suggests a rural bias; the wages in the *chantiers* were very low, and the Quebec power companies, unlike Ontario Hydro, had shown no interest in rural electrification. In any case, an attack on the "trusts" would be popular in rural or urban Quebec; wealthy financiers and industrialists were vulnerable anywhere in Canada during the depression. The A.L.N. policy—the nationalization of the trusts—had a widespread appeal.

The A.L.N. was a popular movement but it failed to change the policies of Taschereau's government. The young reformers, unable to change Taschereau, decided to defeat him. They would run candidates in opposition to the official Liberal candidates at the next election. But what of the Conservative opposition? If both the A.L.N. and the Conservatives ran opposition candidates, the opposition vote would be split and the Liberals would likely win. Paul Gouin, leader of the Action Libérale Nationale, and Maurice Duplessis, leader of the Conservative party, soon got together. A coalition was formed, a coalition which adopted the A.L.N. platform as its program, and Duplessis as its chief. The new party called itself the Union Nationale.

It was an uneasy coalition from the beginning. In the provincial election in 1935 the Union Nationale was remarkably successful, winning 42 of the 90 seats, only a few seats short of a majority. In the previous legislature the opposition had had only 14 seats. The Liberals were still in office but they were clearly losing ground. In the first session of the new Assembly Duplessis quickly established a dominant position. He did so, however, not by advocating the new policies of the A.L.N. but by attacking the government for patronage, nepotism and corruption. Enough evidence was brought to light to convince most people that the Lib-

eral party deserved to be punished. Even Taschereau's
brother, it was discovered, was personally pocketing
the interest on government bank deposits. Taschereau
himself resigned and a new Liberal ministry under
Adélard Godbout called another provincial election in
1936.

Godbout was much more sympathetic to the young
Liberal reformers but by then the die was cast. Paul
Gouin had lost confidence in Duplessis but instead of
returning to the Liberal party he withdrew from politics entirely. His followers in the A.L.N. were successfully wooed by Duplessis and the Union Nationale
coalition survived to win a sweeping victory with 76
of the 90 seats.

Once in office, Maurice Duplessis soon disillusioned
the reformers. His cabinet included only a few of the
prominent A.L.N. members; within a few years the
most radical, or most committed, of the former Liberals
had resigned from the Union Nationale in disgust.
Duplessis did not nationalize the trusts. He did spend
a good deal of money on settlement, roads and rural
services, but he proved to be as reliable a champion of
free enterprise and as good a friend of big business as
Taschereau had ever been. It did surely seem that in
the province of Quebec nothing ever would change:
plus ça change, plus c'est la même chose.

Duplessis's attitude towards the urban proletariat
was illustrated by his Padlock Law. The Padlock Law—
the official title was an Act Respecting Communistic
Propaganda—gave Duplessis the power to lock up any
premises used for "propagating Communism or Bolshe-
vism." The act, however, made no attempt to define
these terms. It could be, and was, used to suppress any
radical agitation among the working class or the unemployed. Many English-Canadian liberals were

shocked at this threat to civil liberties but it was a popular measure in the province of Quebec.

English-speaking Canadians have usually attributed the popularity of this arbitrary measure to the fact that French Canada was Roman Catholic. The assumption was that Roman Catholics have little respect for individual liberties. This, of course, says more about English-Canadian prejudices than it does about Catholicism. The Roman Catholic Church is not a monolithic institution. There were many prominent European Catholics who were deeply concerned with the rights of the working class; there were even many leading Catholics who supported the Republicans in Spain against Franco, even though the communists were supporting the Republicans too. In Quebec, however, there were few left-wing Roman Catholics because there were so few French Canadians who concerned themselves with the problems of urbanization and industrialization. Communists were not exactly popular in English-speaking Canada but at least there were some liberals and socialists who defended the rights of workers to organize and to improve their lot. English Canadians, therefore, were less likely to leap to the conclusion that a protest or a strike was a nefarious communist plot. In Quebec the emphasis was still on rural society. There was so little concern and understanding of industrial problems that any disturbance among workers was readily attributed to alien, communist influence. Thus Duplessis's Padlock Law seemed quite reasonable to most French Canadians. Nor was it unpopular among financiers and industrialists. Duplessis was re-establishing the Taschereau system of winning financial support from the capitalists and voting support from the rural areas.

Duplessis, like Taschereau, also became the champion of provincial rights. The problems of an industrial society had become even more acute during the depression, and the federal government was being forced into taking more and more initiative in economic affairs. The Bennett New Deal included legislation on minimum wages and maximum hours, for example, although in this case the courts decided that the B.N.A. Act did not give the federal government the necessary power to pass such legislation. The constitution would have to be amended before the federal government could act. Maurice Duplessis adamantly refused to consider surrendering any provincial powers. Indeed he was not even prepared to discuss the possibility. When the federal government set up a royal commission—the Rowell-Sirois Commission—to analyse dominion-provincial relations and to suggest reforms, Duplessis denied even the right of the federal government to establish such a commission and refused to submit a provincial brief.

The final act, as far as the 1930s were concerned, came in November of 1939. By then Canada was at war. Duplessis called a snap election, believing that French Canadians were lukewarm about the war effort and convinced that a campaign on the dangers of federal encroachment on provincial rights in wartime would be effective. But he misjudged the situation. The federal Liberals, under Lapointe, took an active part in the election; Duplessis was defeated and Godbout returned to office.

It proved to be a Pyrrhic victory for the Liberals. Godbout did nationalize the largest of the power trusts —the Montreal Light, Heat and Power Company. He also introduced educational reforms, including compulsory education to the age of fourteen. In many ways his policies reflected a growing awareness of the realities of an urban, industrial society. Duplessis, however, was able to establish the image of Godbout as a puppet of the federal government, selling out the interests of the province to the English-Canadian majority in Ottawa. The Union Nationale returned to office in 1944 and the Duplessis system was re-established, a system that survived until after his death in 1959. It was not to be until the 1960s that the provincial governments of Quebec concerned themselves with the problems of an urban and industrial society.

8
Mitchell Hepburn: The Man from the Back Concessions

Mitch Hepburn was the Liberal premier of Ontario from 1934 to 1942. This may not seem remarkable; premiers come and go even in Ontario. Liberal premiers are more exceptional in this province. Mitch was the first Liberal to be elected to that office since 1904, and also the last. What was even more exceptional, however, was that Hepburn was not the kind of person one expects to be chosen for this high office in the staid, stolid and respectable province of Ontario.

Hepburn was brash, bucolic and earthy. He was colourful; he brought a vitality into politics, with his colloquial phrases and his erratic enthusiasm. Vitality can be an asset in politics, but Hepburn's vitality was the hearty, back-slapping and hollow *joie de vivre* of the proverbial travelling salesman. He drank heavily in bars and hotel rooms with shady cronies and he frequently relaxed in the company of women of ill repute instead of his wife. Here for example is a description of Mitch Hepburn by a British visitor to Toronto, a description actually published in the Toronto *Saturday Night* in 1937 when Mitch was Premier of the province.

He had a round cheerful face and neatly brushed hair that grew far back on his forehead and a chin that was small but purposeful. He wore a well-tailored, double-breasted suit and had the appearance and manner of a popular young man-about-town. From the room behind him came the sounds of radio dance music and ice tinkling in glasses and girls' voices....

Mitchell Hepburn led me into the room where the radio was playing, and introduced me to his friends. They were his doctor and a member of his Government and two attractive girls who sprawled on a sofa and called the Prime Minister "Chief"....
A big broad-shouldered fellow with the supple movements of a trained athlete mixed drinks and ...periodically dashed out of the apartment after slipping on a camel-hair coat and a light felt hat with the brim turned up in front.... It was evident that he acted as a sort of bodyguard-cum-gentleman's servant to the Prime Minister. The latter called him "Eddie", but the girls just called him "Bruiser".[1]

It would be difficult to imagine such things being said about any other premier of Ontario, or to believe after such an article appeared that the man could continue to be premier. How was it possible for such a per-

---

[1] Quoted in Neil McKenty, *Mitch Hepburn* (Toronto, 1967), p. 182. This biography is the source of most of the material in this chapter on Hepburn's political career.

son to become premier of the richest and most conservative province of Canada, and a man who, for all his faults, is still remembered with affection and admiration by many of his contemporaries? Obviously there is no simple explanation. The man himself had charm, he had drive and ambition, and he had political ability. But the explanation is also to be found in the times, in the depression of the 1930s, when it seemed that respectable leaders had led the province to disaster and when it seemed time for a change. Hepburn was certainly a change. To explain how Hepburn came to power we must look at the combination of character and circumstances.

Hepburn inherited a prosperous farm near St. Thomas, Ontario. His father had had a traumatic experience in politics, an experience which certainly marked Mitch. Billy Hepburn was campaigning as Liberal candidate back in 1906 when he was accused by his Conservative opponent of having spent one night in a bawdy house. A judge later denounced it as "a foul and most wicked conspiracy" but the damage was done. Hepburn's father withdrew from the race, withdrew from Ontario to try to establish himself in Minnesota and later in Winnipeg and, to put it briefly, failed in all his undertakings. Mitch himself came back as a boy to help on his grandfather's farm, which he eventually inherited, but his father's tragedy left its marks. Mitch was determined to vindicate the family name—to succeed. He also carried with him a continuing mistrust and even hatred of the establishment, of respectable leaders of society who could and would ruin a man to serve their own selfish ends. His cynicism about the traditional elite fitted well into the mood of the 1930s when it seemed clear that these leaders had failed.

How did Hepburn become leader of the provincial

Liberal party in the first place? He was first elected as a federal Liberal M.P. in 1926. He was then thirty years old but he was already cocky and aggressive. He was an effective and dynamic speaker but he resented discipline and had little respect for his seniors in the party. He was re-elected in 1930 but was then asked by some dissident provincial Liberals to contest the provincial leadership. Mackenzie King tried to dissuade him. King did not want Hepburn to resign his federal seat—it might be won by a Conservative in the ensuing by-election—but he was also dubious about a man of Hepburn's type as party leader. King, after all, was himself respectable, abstemious, and correct. Hepburn, however, paid no attention to King. He had no respect for old fogies.

Hepburn was a protest candidate, protesting against the domination of upper-class Toronto and Sinclair, the incumbent leader. Sinclair had lost two elections on a prohibition platform and although he had called the convention he was expected to be a candidate. Hepburn was the antithesis of this stodgy, elderly, dull and pessimistic leader; Hepburn on the platform roused emotions and attacked the Tories with biting partisanship. In contrast to his dry opponent, Hepburn was, as one of his acquaintances wrote, "too wet to burn." His enthusiastic reception at the convention disillusioned Sinclair, who refused to run, and Hepburn became leader of the Ontario Liberal party in 1930 at the age of thirty-four.

He was not enthusiastically supported by all Liberals. Mackenzie King could accept the inevitable gracefully; he wired his congratulations to Hepburn and asked other Ontario Liberals to support their new leader. Sinclair's reply to this appeal is revealing. For Sinclair loyalty to the party had its limits.

You suggest that I aid Hepburn. I do not see how

I can be of much assistance. His friends are not my friends. Whatever faults I may have, I know he is of a much inferior type of mind to my own.... His chief qualifications consist in making rabid speeches, one sentence of which at any time may be his undoing. [2]

Hepburn was clearly a gamble, and many prominent Liberals were not yet gamblers.

Over the next four years Mitch Hepburn showed an exuberant energy and a dynamism that were unusual in Ontario politics. The Liberal party, out of office for thirty years, was a minority party. Under Hepburn it attracted support from large segments of the population that, during the depression, felt themselves neglected and ignored by the government at Queen's Park. Hepburn, himself a farmer, could easily pose as a champion of rural Ontario; he had once been a member of the United Farmers of Ontario, the farmers' party which had actually been in office in the early 1920s. Hepburn himself had no direct contact with labour, with new Canadians or with Roman Catholics, the other groups who had grievances and who felt excluded from the ruling class of the province. He inspired confidence, however, because he was so clearly anti-establishment, and also because he was soon supported by such men as Arthur Roebuck and David Croll, both of whom had the confidence and respect of workers and immigrants, and by Peter Heenan, a prominent Irish Catholic. By 1934, therefore, Hepburn was the leader of a new coalition, a coalition which included farm, labour, ethnic and Catholic support.

It was not clear at this stage whether Hepburn really was a reformer. He used the rhetoric of reform. He talked

[2] Mackenzie King Papers, W.E.N. Sinclair to W.L.M. King, December 30, 1930.

of the rights of labour, the rights of the underprivileged, the rights of the people, the need for increased relief and public works. His campaign, however, was primarily an attack on the Tory government and the nefarious influences of Big Business, which he insisted was exploiting the province. Attacks on anonymous but subversive financial manipulators are always appropriate speech material in an election campaign; they were even more effective in 1934 when wealthy businessmen were such an obvious target and such convenient scapegoats for a depression for which somebody must be responsible. Hepburn's homespun vitriol was thus applauded by his audiences.

But Hepburn went beyond generalizations; he concentrated his attack on hydroelectric power corporations. The ground had already been prepared. In the United States the private power companies were being bitterly attacked for exploiting the poor and corrupting the powerful. The Beauharnois Power Corporation in Canada had become infamous for the huge profits of its promoters and for its financial contributions to the federal Liberal party. Hepburn specifically charged that prominent Tories, including Arthur Meighen and Premier George Henry, had personally benefited from political concessions to private firms and from power contracts negotiated by the provincial government. There was some fire behind all the smoke. A private company in northern Ontario had defaulted on its bond payments whereupon the government had arranged to have Ontario Hydro take over power sites owned by this company. The bonds of the company were quickly restored to their original market value. There was nothing so exceptional about this except that both Meighen, an Ontario Hydro Commissioner, and Premier Henry had owned some of these bonds. Meighen, in fact, had sold his bonds when he became

Commissioner but Henry admitted that he had $25,000 worth of bonds which he had forgotten. To forget sums of this magnitude, especially during the depression, was not politically astute, to say the least. Hepburn, however, was not overly concerned with facts. He was prepared to believe and to accuse his opponents of the worst. Here is his description of George Henry, Premier of Ontario, in one of his campaign speeches.

> Honest George they call him, and Charlie Mc-Crea says he hasn't a dishonest hair in his head. That's fair enough because he's bald....Why honest George is the man who forgot he had 25,000 tucked away in Abitibi bonds. He forgot he was a director of a company that had 200,000 in it, and he forgot the Right Honourable Arthur Meighen's companies had 300,000 invested in it.... I feel sorry for Honest George. All he has is about a million or so that he made out of Acme Dairy. If any of you farmers water your milk you go to jail. But if you water your stock you get to be Premier of Ontario. [3]

This was typical of Hepburn's campaign. He did not bother to present a platform or to elaborate his policies. He was the accuser, accusing the government of incapacity, of lack of sympathy and concern for the common people, of personal greed and corruption. It was an appeal to emotions; the appeal of a demagogue. It was effective because people were prepared to believe the worst of the traditional political leaders and were prepared to believe the best of this brash, flamboyant, young upstart who had the courage to denounce them. In 1934 young Mitch Hepburn won the election. He had led his party after thirty years in the

[3] Quoted in McKenty, *op. cit.,* p. 56.

wilderness to the seats of the mighty, the greatest Liberal victory in the history of the province: 66 Liberal seats with only 17 Conservative survivors. The people of Ontario, predicted George Henry, were in for interesting times.

Mitch was as flamboyant in office as out of office. He had promised retrenchment and he publicized his economies with a flair. For example, he held a public auction for the official cars which had been provided at public expense for Tory ministers and dignitaries. He cut the salaries of civil servants and dismissed all those hired within the last year. It did not matter that many new appointments soon had to be made and that the new civil servants were likely to be Liberals; it was the dramatic gesture that was remembered. Most dramatic of all was Hepburn's refusal to honour four large power contracts. These contracts with private power companies in Quebec, including Beauharnois, dated back to 1929 when Ontario Hydro had foreseen a shortage of power for the province and had negotiated long-range contracts with these companies to supply fixed amounts of power over a forty-year period. By 1934 there was no shortage of power—the depression had seen to that—but the contracts had been signed. Hepburn simply passed a law which cancelled the contracts. There was no legal justification for welshing on this obligation, but few people lost any sleep over this arbitrary treatment of private power companies. Nor did it seem to matter that within a few years Ontario actually needed additional power and that Hepburn's government renegotiated these contracts. In spite of all this Mitch Hepburn was more than ever "the people's choice," even if orthodox and respectable businessmen had their doubts.

But governing is more than a theatrical art. There

was a depression and the government had to meet the
problems it created. The immediate need was to provide relief in the form of food, clothing and shelter for
the unemployed and the impoverished and their families. The long-range aim of restoring full employment and prosperity could not conceal the absolute
necessity of finding money for this relief in the meantime. Dramatic economies and cancelled contracts
were not enough. The Ontario government had to find
more money. It also had to meet the changing social conditions which the depression helped to create. Hepburn's problems and his reactions to them can be illustrated by two major issues: the Oshawa strike of 1937,
and his feud with Mackenzie King. In each case Hepburn was vehement and vituperative, but in each case
his reaction showed him to be conservative and traditional in his outlook. For all his dynamism and
bluster, Mitchell Hepburn was not a radical or even
a social reformer. He had little sympathy for change
and no understanding of modern society.

The Oshawa strike was probably the turning point
in Hepburn's political career. Hepburn's cavalier can-
cellation of the power contracts had disturbed the
business community and when the province of Ontario
had to borrow money, as inevitably it did, the response
of bankers was almost hostile. The wealthy men who
did rally around Hepburn were those who could benefit directly from a political alliance: the mining magnates such as Sir James Dunn of Algoma Steel, J. P.
Bickell and Sell'em Ben Smith, and George McCullagh who had made a fortune in northern Ontario
mining investments and now owned the Toronto *Globe
and Mail*. These men were rich but they were not yet
part of the financial establishment. They were speculators, promoters, plungers, and not quite respect-

able; but they did have influence and contacts on Bay Street and Wall Street. Hepburn needed their help, and he got it because he had something to offer in return. (Sir James Dunn, for example, received a subsidy on iron-ore production.) But the association was more than a business relationship. These men and their hangers-on became Hepburn's buddies, his company on drinking parties and on high-flying holidays in the United States. George McCullagh also became his personal financial adviser and invested money for him in promising mining stocks. More and more, the onion farmer from St. Thomas became identified with speculators and acquisitive mining magnates.

These new associations help to account for Hepburn's splenetic reaction to the Oshawa strike. The roots of the strike are to be found in the United States with the formation of the C.I.O. (the Congress of Industrial Organization) under John L. Lewis. The old American Federation of Labor was a federation of craft unions, with workers in each trade or craft having their own union. This traditional form of association was outdated by the new techniques of mass production. Organized workers in a single industry were divided into a number of separate trade unions and so their bargaining power was greatly reduced. At the same time, unskilled workers were not organized at all. The C.I.O. advocated organization by industry rather than by craft, so that all miners or all automobile workers would be united in a single powerful union. Businessmen were naturally unsympathetic to a new form of trade unionism which would give labour more bargaining power. Lack of sympathy, however, was transmuted into fear by the conviction that the C.I.O. was dominated by radicals—by communists—who wanted to destroy the capitalist system. Events seemed to confirm this fear, for the newly organized C.I.O. unions in the United States were aggressive and militant. Under these circumstances it was not surprising that violence erupted. Police were called in against strikers; the strikers themselves took the law into their own hands and occupied factories illegally in sit-down strikes. It was easy for the advocates of law and order to believe that the C.I.O. was a subversive and revolutionary organization.

It was inevitable that the C.I.O. would spread into Canada. The United Auto Workers could hardly be expected to stop at the border when U.S. corporations like General Motors did not. Thus in 1937 the majority of the workers at the General Motors plant in Oshawa formed a local of the C.I.O. and opened negotiations with the plant management. At this stage there was nothing unusual about the situation. The issues were the common issues of union recognition, higher wages and better working conditions. Management refused to recognize the affiliation of the union with the C.I.O. but was prepared to negotiate with the workers' representatives.

The situation became critical because the provincial government intervened. Until then Hepburn had shown no great interest in labour problems. He came from a rural environment and had a farmer's suspicion of the demands of organized labour. He also had a humanitarian concern for the underprivileged, however, and the presence of Arthur Roebuck and David Croll in his cabinet had given the impression of a government which was sympathetic to labour. When negotiations broke down in Oshawa, Croll as Minister of Labour quite consistently insisted on the right of the workers to affiliate with the C.I.O. if they chose to do so. Hepburn, however, had a different reaction. He had declared that he would not tolerate sit-down strikes in Ontario and that his government would maintain law and order at all costs. In spite of assurances by the union leaders and by the mayor of Oshawa that there was no violence and that no sit-down strike was contemplated, Hepburn took action. He called Ottawa for R.C.M.P. reinforcements. He recruited four hundred special constables—university students and veterans promptly dubbed "Hepburn's Hussars." He issued a statement to the effect that American communist revolutionaries were threatening to take over Canadian industries but that he was prepared for a showdown.

Why did Hepburn react so violently? In part it was the combination of communist and American influences which he saw as responsible for disrupting the tranquillity of law-abiding Ontario. Because he had little understanding of or sympathy for trade unions he could not imagine that the industrial conditions which had produced the C.I.O. in the United States might produce a similar movement in Canada. It was easy for him to blame alien subversives for all the trouble. Nor was Hepburn alone in this. Most of the citizens of Ontario were antagonistic to militant labour, especially citizens from rural Ontario or from the respectable middle class. It was easy for them to believe the worst. And what could be worse than the nefarious influence of communist or American agitators? Hepburn was undoubtedly supported by the majority of people in the province.

But Hepburn's intemperate reaction also had other roots. Industrial unionism in the United States was not confined to the automobile industry; it was also strong in the mining industry. Hepburn's cronies thus had special reasons for an immediate showdown with the C.I.O. because if it succeeded at Oshawa it would soon move north into the mines. George McCullagh in the *Globe and Mail* was almost hysterical. Hepburn's statements followed the *Globe and Mail* line, often word for word.

In the end the Oshawa strike was settled without violence. The local union got its contract although it did not get official recognition of its C.I.O. affiliation. Both the workers and the government could claim a victory. But the Oshawa strike was a turning point in Hepburn's career. Workers could no longer believe that he was a reformer. During the strike he had demanded the resignation of Arthur Roebuck and David Croll, the two ministers in his government who were openly sympathetic to labour. From then on Hepburn and his government were more and more identified with big business; the fiery radical had turned out to be conservative.

The other major event was the feud between Hepburn and Mackenzie King. There is always tension between federal and provincial governments in our federal system, and when two levels of government operate within the same territory there are bound to be controversies. The disputes usually focus on financial matters for good reason. No government can operate effectively if it does not have large enough revenues to carry out its responsibilities. In our federal system, however, the national and the provincial governments both collect taxes from the same taxpayers. There are endless opportunities for friction and rivalry.

The depression aggravated the situation although the roots of the problem go back to the B.N.A. Act of 1867. The Fathers of Confederation thought of provincial governments as local governments with only local responsibilities. In those days roads were local because vehicles were horse-drawn, social welfare was local because each local community accepted responsibility for its indigents, education was local because the local schoolhouse provided an education that was adequate for rural communities. Thus roads, welfare and education were entrusted to provincial governments. But with industrialization and urbanization, these responsibilities became more significant and more onerous. Cars and trucks needed better roads; the unemployed, the aged and the weak needed government aid; citizens needed a more sophisticated education. Provincial governments responded to these new demands. They were able to afford the increasing expenditures in prosperous times because the direct taxes which the B.N.A. Act allowed them to collect on property, liquor and gasoline were lucrative sources of income. Provinces usually had deficits and provincial debts mounted but their credit rating was good, and the money for expanding services could be found.

The depression shattered the precarious balance between provincial expenditures and provincial revenues. Welfare payments for the unemployed spiralled and revenues from direct taxes plummeted. Provincial credit was no longer sound, and some provincial governments were unable to borrow money. Their only hope was to get money from the federal government. The western provinces were the hardest hit. Wheat farmers were faced with recurring crop failures and even if they harvested a crop the price of wheat was so low that they were scarcely better off. Since farmers could not pay taxes under these conditions but had to be given relief, money had to come from the federal government.

The province of Ontario suffered less. The drought was less serious and the farmers of Ontario could grow some of their own food; there was serious unemployment but many factories continued to operate at reduced levels. In the northern mines there was even some expansion. Even in Ontario, however, the demands on the provincial government spiralled. This was complicated by the fact that the federal government had to subsidize the governments of the prairie provinces to prevent them from going bankrupt, and the money had to come from federal taxes, most of which were collected from the people and corporations in central Canada. Not surprisingly there were objections to these transfer payments. Ontario and Quebec would be better off if the money they paid in taxes was returned to them instead of being spent in western Canada.

This was a selfish and short-sighted view of the situation. No provincial economy was a separate unit. The industries of Ontario, for example, were dependent upon markets outside the province, so that employment in Ontario depended upon recovery in other parts of Canada. It was true, however, that not all sectors of Ontario's economy were affected by developments in other parts of Canada. Some industries, such as the pulp and paper and the mining industries, produced for the U.S. rather than the Canadian market. Thus the concept of an integrated national economy, the basis of the National Policy dating back to the days of John A. Macdonald, was being undermined by this continental outlook. The sense of a Canadian community, of common interests, was weakened by a north-south orientation.

This constitutional and economic background is only part of the story. The personalities of Hepburn and Mackenzie King, the respective heads of the governments of Ontario and of Canada, added an important dimension. The two men were complete opposites. Hepburn was convivial, roistering, emotional, flamboyant, undignified; King was staid, controlled, calculating, and very proper and conven-

tional. Neither of them liked or trusted the other.
Under some circumstances this would not have mat-
tered; after all they belonged to the same political
party and the bond of party can survive many strains.
Certainly King was prepared to make concessions; he
was always prepared to make concessions. He would
be cautious and guarded but publicly at least he would
be correct and proper and even cordial. Not so Hepburn; he could not conceal his feelings and in times of
stress he publicized them.

It would be too long a story to trace the relations
between the two men. Their mistrust of each other had
been obvious at the time of the Ontario Liberal convention which chose Hepburn, and it was never dispelled.
The provincial and federal wings of the party co-
operated in the Ontario election of 1934 that brought
Hepburn to office, and in the federal election of 1935
that brought King to office. Indeed, Hepburn campaigned across Canada for King in that election. But
even then the relations were uneasy.

As an example of this, when Hepburn was elected,
King wrote to congratulate him and to offer him any
assistance he might want. Always circumspect, however, King made it clear that he had no intention of
interfering. Hepburn was the Premier of Ontario and
the decisions at the provincial level must be his alone.
In 1935, however, Hepburn tried to push King into
giving a cabinet position to one of Hepburn's friends.
He received a very polite but a very firm no; King quite
properly insisted on choosing his own cabinet. Hepburn, who had worked so hard to get King elected, was
less impressed by constitutional proprieties. He took it
as a personal insult when his candidate was not
appointed.

Inevitably, there were many other issues on which
King felt unable to do what Hepburn wanted him to do:

King would not allow the export of waterpower to the United States, he was reluctant to provide R.C.M.P. for the Oshawa strike, he gave Ontario smaller relief grants than Hepburn demanded. The federal government could hardly be expected to satisfy all the demands of a provincial government. Given the contrast in personalities and Hepburn's volatility, however, each new incident only added fuel to what Hepburn soon saw as a personal feud. In every case King was at his tactful best. He was meticulous about the formalities, went out of his way to explain his own position and refused to react to ultimatums or insults. But King was also firm; he offered only compromises or concessions. In each case Hepburn was confirmed in his conviction that King was dithering and indecisive, a schemer and a coward. An open breach was almost inevitable.

The breach might have come in 1937 when Hepburn publicly declared that he was a Liberal, but not a Mackenzie King Liberal. It might have come a few months later when Hepburn exploded with the accusation: "Mr. King was never friendly to Ontario. I happen to know because I was with him and watched him in Ottawa." It might have come when Hepburn formed an informal alliance with Maurice Duplessis against the federal government, and when the two men virtually declared war against King. Indeed, for three years, Mitch Hepburn seemed to be trying deliberately to provoke King to retaliate. The impetuous Mitch had turned Ontario's relations with Ottawa into a personal feud, and open war between the two Liberal leaders was only avoided because King insisted on turning the other cheek. He made no public references to Hepburn's personal attacks and concentrated on presenting the federal side of the story as reasonably as possible.

In the long run, it was clear that Mitch came out second best. His verbal excesses, his exaggerations and his undignified behaviour diminished his stature. King's behaviour was typical. He seethed inside over Hepburn's attacks but he gave no outward sign. He was sure that Hepburn would destroy himself, and he did not intend to go down with him. It is even probable that King knew that his own restraint would encourage Hepburn to further excesses.

The breach finally came in 1940. It came when King decided that it was safe and personally advantageous to go on to the offensive. At the outbreak of war, Hepburn was more than ever sure that King must go. Such a pusillanimous prime minister was not fit to be a wartime leader. In 1940 he went so far as to move a resolution in the Ontario Legislature to regret that "the Federal Government at Ottawa has made so little effort to prosecute Canada's duty in the war in the vigorous manner the people of Canada desire to see." The leader of the Ontario opposition, George Drew, seconded the resolution.

Mackenzie King eagerly took up the gauntlet this time. There had to be a federal election in that year. King seized the occasion to dissolve Parliament abruptly and to go to the people for a vote of confidence in his leadership. He appealed to the loyalty of patriotic Canadians who wanted to keep Canada united in its war effort. His critics were put on the defensive. Hepburn misjudged the situation. He accused King of scuttling the ship of state instead of prosecuting the war. By this time, however, even his friend George McCullagh of the *Globe and Mail* was disgusted with Hepburn's personal attacks on the federal government, and many of Hepburn's own colleagues campaigned for federal Liberal candidates. Ontario voted solidly Liberal; King's government was returned with an overwhelming majority.

The showdown had finally come. King and the federal government had won and Mitch Hepburn had been destroyed. Within two years he had resigned, a broken man and, in 1943, at the next provincial election even his own constituents rejected him. The Hepburn era was ended in Ontario.

9
"Bible Bill" Aberhart and Armageddon in Alberta

In August of the year 1935 Canadians, and indeed people far beyond Canadian borders, wondered if the electors of Alberta had taken leave of their senses. The radio quickly spread the news across the continents that the voters in this remote province had overwhelmingly approved the lunatic ideas of a certain Major Douglas and had elected to office the first Social Credit government in the world. Was it a portent of where the world was heading as a result of the depression? Was it true, as one cartoonist suggested, that Alberta was the little child who would lead them? Or had Albertans suddenly gone mad and, like lemmings, leapt to mass self-destruction? Observers looked for a simple apocalyptic explanation for the incredible election results. That was their mistake. There was no simple answer.

The Social Credit movement began in Alberta in 1932. It was not even a political movement until 1935. By August of that year, however, Social Credit candidates had been nominated in every constituency and of the 63 candidates, 56 were elected. There could be no easy and simple explanation for such an upheaval in the political structure of the province. The depression was part of the story; its disastrous impact helped to explain why new and radical and untried policies were taken seriously. But it must also be remembered that Saskatchewan and Manitoba were suffering from the depression as well, but the voters there did not turn to Social Credit. Alberta was not a province like the others. It had turned away from the old parties as early as 1920 and had kept the United Farmers of Alberta in office for fifteen years. And Alberta also had "Bible Bill" Aberhart, the prophet and the general of the crusading army of Social Credit. Aberhart is clearly central to any explanation of the 1935 election results. But how was it that an evangelist like Aberhart had already become one of the best-known citizens of the province even before he turned to politics? What made Alberta such fertile soil for this prophet of religious and then of political salvation?

The Alberta election of 1935 was clearly a remarkable conjuncture of events: an economic crisis, a political vacuum, the intervention of a dynamic evangelist in politics. These separate factors coincided at a crucial moment, and their combination produced a maelstrom which swept away existing political structures and left Aberhart and his Social Credit movement in their place. To understand this conjuncture we must trace the separate currents and see how they merged in 1935.

The depression was the mainstream. Alberta, like the other prairie provinces, was quite unable to cope with the crisis. It was a predominantly rural province, producing grain and cattle, with even the towns and cities existing primarily to serve the farm population. When the price of farm products dropped everybody in Alberta was affected. Who could prosper when choice steers, weighing a thousand pounds, were selling in Calgary in the fall of 1932 for $22.50? Farm prices did not meet the costs of production. When drought and rust and frost destroyed grain and hay crops a situation which had been desperate became impossible. Alberta farmers and those who served them faced disaster; they had become completely dependent on outside help, on the charity of the federal government and of Canadians outside the province.

This was also true in the other prairie provinces. Alberta differed to some extent because many regions of Alberta were the last sections of the prairies to be settled. This meant that the debt burden of mortgages was slightly higher; the newer farms had not been paid for. Mortgages were significant because farmers could not meet their payments; they could not even pay off the interest, much less the capital. The insecurity of farmers, whose debts were increasing and who had no legal protection against foreclosure, was a potent factor in creating a mood of political desperation. But the difference between the mood of the farmers in Alberta and that of farmers in the other prairie provinces must not be exaggerated. In each province the time was ripe for a political upheaval. The depression does not explain why the upheaval in Alberta took the unique form of Social Credit.

Another difference was Alberta's distinctive political experience, with roots going back many years. The prairies have always believed that they were being exploited. Eastern Canada has been the villain; by the east, westerners mean the industrial and financial heartland which includes both Toronto and Montreal.

The place of Quebec in Confederation, fear of American domination, and other issues which have played a significant part in political controversies elsewhere in Canada have never aroused much concern on the prairies. From the beginning, the west concentrated on its economic problems, and all too often the east seemed to be to blame for western difficulties. Prairie wheat has to be exported and so railway freight rates are a major expense but, as far as prairie farmers are concerned, freight rates are high because they are controlled by eastern railway magnates and by eastern politicians. Tariffs are seen as another example of eastern exploitation. Eastern politicians had established protective tariffs for the benefit of eastern manufacturers, at the expense of westerners who buy the manufactured goods. Banks and mortgage companies also have their headquarters in eastern Canada, and to western farmers this explained why banks would not lend money to them during the depression, and why mortgage companies continued to demand their pound of flesh, with the ever-present menace of foreclosure. To many westerners the major political parties, Conservative and Liberal, were an integral part of this system of exploiting the west for the benefit of the east. These parties were financed by eastern industrialists and financiers and, so it was argued, were the corrupted tools of "Big Business." Even the Liberal party, for all its talk of lower tariffs and freer trade, seemed suspiciously reluctant to do anything which would alienate these vested interests in eastern Canada.

This western grievance, this sense of exploitation, had come to the fore in the brief depression immediately after the war. The Progressive movement had been primarily a western farmers' movement, committed to the aim of having farmers take political power into their own hands. The Progressives came into office in Manitoba in 1922. Manitoba Progressives, however, were relatively moderate. Winnipeg, after all, was a railway and a commercial and financial centre, the metropolis of western Canada, and its prosperity was linked to the National Policy. John Bracken, the Progressive leader, was no doctrinaire, and in 1932 he formed a coalition with the provincial Liberals and supported the federal Liberals at the federal level. In Saskatchewan, the provincial Liberal party had stayed in office in the early 1920s by absorbing the leaders of farmers' organizations. It had been defeated in 1929 by a coalition of Conservatives and anti-Liberal Progressives. By the next provincial election, in 1934, the reaction against the government, including the anti-Liberal Progressives, was so extreme that the Liberals under Jimmy Gardiner were swept back into office.

Alberta was different. There too the Progressive movement had mushroomed immediately after the war and the United Farmers of Alberta had been elected to office in 1920. In Alberta, however, there were no moderating factors as there were in Manitoba, and Alberta Progressives were more radical, less prepared to compromise with financial and industrial interests. They talked about economic classes, with farmers engaged in a struggle against vested interests. Another difference was that the provincial Liberal party, discredited by a railway scandal, was much weaker than the Liberal party in Saskatchewan. Thus even in the 1920s Alberta was unique, with its own distinctive political experience, more radical, more separated from the mainstream of Canadian politics. The difference shows up at the federal level as well. Progressives had been elected to the House of Commons from each of the prairie provinces in 1921 and again in 1925, but by 1926 the Progressives in Manitoba and Saskatchewan were back in the Liberal fold. Only the United Farmers of Alberta maintained their distinctive identity and even in the federal election of 1930, nine of the sixteen M.P.s elected from Alberta were U.F.A. members.

By 1935, therefore, Alberta was already something of a maverick province. For fifteen years it had consistently supported, both federally and provincially, a political party which was distinctive and unique. What was more, not only had Albertans become more and more separated from the major political parties, but by this time even the United Farmers party was under a cloud. To begin with it had been in office for fifteen years, the last five years during the depression. This in itself was enough to alienate some of its support; it was bound to be blamed for the depression by some voters. The party was also weakened by the founding of the new C.C.F. party, a socialist party which included the remnants of the farmers' parties in the other provinces. As the party in office, it would be risky for the U.F.A. to change its name, even though many of its leaders were sympathetic to the new party. It therefore maintained its identity but undoubtedly suffered from its indecision and ambivalence. The U.F.A. could not benefit from the enthusiasm and optimism of the new C.C.F. party and yet it was close enough to the C.C.F. to suffer from the accusation of being socialist.

Finally, there was a scandal; and not a scandal over mere money, but a much more serious scandal—a moral scandal. The leader of the U.F.A. and premier of the province was accused of seducing his housemaid. People who knew Mr. Brownlee were absolutely certain that it was a frame-up but the courts awarded damages to the maid. Brownlee resigned but the stigma of immorality remained. It was a hard blow for a party whose *raison d'être* had been the corruption of the old-line parties.

The loss of faith in the U.F.A. party, both because it had failed to resolve the problems of the depression and because it had fallen from grace, did not restore faith in the old Conservative and Liberal parties. These parties, in Alberta at least, had been on the fringe of political activity for fifteen years and appeared more than ever to be mere appendages of the federal parties, stooges of the vested interests of the east. The decline of the U.F.A. therefore meant a kind of political vacuum in which no party had a positive appeal.

It was at this conjuncture that Social Credit appeared. But to understand why it appeared and why it raised genuine enthusiasm and won widespread allegiance, we must go back in time to trace the career of the prophet and salesman extraordinary, William Aberhart.

Aberhart was a Calgary high-school principal. He was a very efficient administrator: teachers had their timetables, students knew the regulations and all went smoothly. He was also a successful teacher in the sense that students learned to pass their exams. There were criticisms of his methods. One member of his staff, for example, claimed that students memorized but they did not learn and that if a student showed any independence he was frightened into submission.

Aberhart, he said, was a good dog-trainer, or perhaps we should say a good drill-master. He wanted his students to learn their tricks mechanically, and never mind the *reason* for them. His rule-of-thumb approach which led him to use charts in teaching arithmetic, got them through the examinations, but when it was all over they hadn't the faintest idea *why* they had answered the questions that way. He insisted on mechanical memory, without thought or reasoning behind it.[1]

Aberhart was not sensitive to criticism. He considered himself and was considered by most parents to be a very successful teacher. But Aberhart was a man of tremendous energy and probably also had a tremendous need to dominate, to impose his will. By the mid-1920s he was not only running a very popular Baptist Bible class at Westbourne Church in Calgary, but he had also become the preacher, giving two sermons each Sunday to a growing congregation, and for the weekdays he had a Bible Institute, a fundamentalist Bible college. The most significant step, however, came when Aberhart was persuaded to broadcast his Sunday afternoon sermons over a pioneer radio station in Calgary. Aberhart proved to be a phenomenally successful broadcaster. He had a clear, sonorous voice, a pleasant voice which he used almost instrumentally, with a wide range of volume and mood to convey his message.

The message was biblical prophecy. Aberhart was a fundamentalist, preaching the revealed word of God. Like other religious sects, Aberhart and his adherents used the Bible to protest against the evils of the modern, materialistic world: the evils of sophisticated academics and their biblical criticism, the cold formality of middle-class congregations, the vices of dancing and movies and drink. The old-fashioned, traditional Christian rejected these evils, rejected the material world with its pride and its temptations, and gave him-

---

[1]John A. Irving, *The Social Credit Movement in Alberta* (Toronto, 1959), pp. 15-16.

self completely and enthusiastically to God. Basical-
ly it was a simple and appealing message: the world
is sinful but Jesus saves.

In the 1920s Aberhart was only one of many fundamentalist preachers in Alberta. Indeed, one sociologist
describes the province as being unique in Canada for
its bewildering mixture of non-conformist religions.
Alberta has its pockets of old-world sects, such as Men-
nonites and Hutterites. Immigrants from the United
States brought with them or later imported an aston-
ishing variety of Apostolic and Pentecostal sects.
Aberhart with his Prophetic Bible Institute was only
one of thirty or forty sects, with each congregation
upholding variations of the same fundamentalist faith,
and each prospering or declining according to the ef-
fectiveness or popularity of its leader.

Radio was a new and significant instrument in en-
larging the congregation of an evangelist. By the end
of the 1920s the isolation of most farm homes had
been pierced by crystal radio sets. There were no net-
works but in Alberta local stations could reach most
of the province and were spared competition from
British Columbia stations because of the Rockies and
from eastern Canadian stations because of distance.
Aberhart was a talented preacher and Alberta was
fertile soil for his message. Radio provided the ideal
medium to cultivate a provincial congregation.

Aberhart also used his talents as an organizer to
good advantage. His radio audience was not composed
of passive listeners. His Radio Sunday School included
a free correspondence course of fifty-two lessons with
exams and prizes. Adults belonged to a radio club and
responded generously to Aberhart's appeals for financial support. It was not long before the Prophetic
Bible Institute had a new building and the mortgage
was paid off. By 1929 Aberhart had a Bible class fol-

lowing in Calgary of seven hundred, with a thousand rural supporters and a radio Sunday School of seven hundred. It was not a phenomenal number but it did mean that Aberhart had established probably the largest individual congregation in Alberta. In addition to these active members there were also people, numbering in the thousands, who tuned in regularly to hear Aberhart's Sunday broadcasts.

Then in 1932 came the significant shift. Aberhart could not have been unaware of the depression: his students could not find jobs; his congregation and his radio audience reduced their donations. Aberhart was undoubtedly moved by the plight of students and adherents. In 1932 he heard about Major Douglas's theory of Social Credit. It was a simple, fundamentalist message; it offered economic salvation to the depressed if only the people would believe. Aberhart's broadcasts on biblical prophecy began to include references to economic problems and questions about the importance of purchasing power and the possible benefits of Social Credit.

In a rural society with prices of farm products at an unprecedented low, and in a debtor society burdened by mortgages, any inflationary scheme looked attractive. When William Aberhart, the respected man of God, talked of inflation, his views carried authority. And when Aberhart applied his talents as teacher and preacher to presenting a simple but dogmatic exposition of Social Credit—so lucid that all could understand, so obvious that all could believe, so sincere that to doubt was almost a sin—it was then that Social Credit became a movement.

Social Credit, or at least Aberhart's version, was simple in the extreme. Major Douglas was an English engineer with an unbounded confidence in technology. Modern technology could provide an era of plenty for all; the fault lay with the few powerful men who controlled the monetary system and reaped the benefits at the expense of the majority. Total purchasing power, according to Douglas, always fell short of the total price of all goods produced, so that for some people there was always poverty in the midst of plenty. The solution was to create enough new money to bring purchasing power and the total cost of goods into balance. This new money was to be distributed in the form of social credit dividends.

This deceptively simple theory raised frighteningly complex problems. What was meant by total purchasing power? How could the social credit be measured? Major Douglas was fuzzy when it came to these refinements. Aberhart, however, was very clear. Credit was like blood; blood flows from the heart, feeds every cell, picks up the impurities, is purified in the lungs and returns to the heart. Every hour, said Aberhart, the heart pumps 135 gallons of blood, over 3,000 gallons a day, over one million gallons a year.

> Where am I going to get all the blood, he asked, will you tell me that? As a matter of fact, I believe I only have four quarts of blood in me, just about four quarts. Will you tell me how a heart can pump 135 gallons an hour with only four quarts of blood? Well, cannot money circulate the same?[2]

Aberhart made it all sound so simple. Pump a little money into the system, make it circulate and there would be plenty for all. Aberhart was also much more specific than Douglas had ever been. There was no need for elaborate statistical calculations to establish how much new money was needed to balance purchas-

[2]Irving, *op. cit.,* p. 117.

ing power and the total cost of goods produced. Out of his hat came the figure of $25 a month for every man and woman in Alberta.

> The fault lies with distribution. It's no good side-tracking the issue, we are just wasting our time looking for any further wrong when we know Distribution is the whole cause. What is the remedy?...Social Credit with its basic dividend to every man and woman of $25.00 per month starts out with the corrective measures at once. It places purchasing power in the hands of the consumer. We have found a scientific way out of our troubles, and if we don't do it, then nobody else will.... Where does all the money come from? We don't use money. Then where does all the credit come from? Why out of the end of a fountain pen.... Social Credit is without doubt the solution to our present economic chaos of poverty in the midst of plenty.[3]

This was the fundamentalist preacher in politics. But Aberhart was also an organizer. Study groups were set up wherever radio listeners responded; the appeal of the new gospel of Social Credit is suggested by the estimate that by 1935 Aberhart's Sunday broadcasts had a total audience of 350,000, including some in Saskatchewan, and in neighbouring states to the south. Bible study groups became Social Credit clubs, pamphlets were distributed, study groups were formed. At the peak of the movement there were sixty-three groups in Calgary alone, and an estimated total of sixteen hundred groups in the province as a whole. This fantastic mushroom growth would not have been possible if Aberhart had not already had a radio au-

[3]*Ibid.*, p. 114.

dience of converts and also if the new gospel of Social Credit had not appeared as the answer to the economic prayers of Albertans during the depression. These study groups were the grass-roots structure of a political party even before Aberhart announced late in 1934 that he wanted Social Credit candidates to run in every constituency in the next election.

Once in the field, the campaign was a triumphal procession. Towering over all the converts, however, was Aberhart himself. Prospective candidates only became official Social Credit candidates after Aberhart's approval. He was the final authority: for the platform, for the strategy, for everything. He was also the dominant individual in the campaign. He drew the crowds and on Sundays he drew the listeners and "with Douglas in one hand and the Holy Ghost in the other," he smote the unbelievers hip and thigh. When election day came the voting was heavy and more than half of the electors proved to be converts to the new movement. The rest of the votes were divided between U.F.A., Liberal and Conservative candidates. It was a landslide, with only 7 opposition members elected to an Assembly of 63. The comments of some of the voters in this election illustrate graphically the many factors which, when combined, account for the stunning results.

First of all there was the depression, the debts which could not be paid and the utter helplessness and hopelessness of the situation. As one farmer recounted:

> Ninety-five per cent of the farm homes in my district were loaded down to an impossible position with debts to the banks and mortgages and machine companies and even to the storekeepers in local villages.... Every week when I went to the post-office, I got a bunch of dunners [bills]. I took

these home in my wagon six miles unopened and
gave them to my wife to open. She opened them because she had more pluck than I had.[4]

There was also the political vacuum, the loss of faith
in the U.F.A. government and in the old-line parties.
As one young man on voting day announced: "Well I
guess Social Credit's no darn good, but who's there to
vote for anyway—I guess I'll vote for Social Credit
anyway."[5] Then there was Aberhart. "I didn't understand Social Credit theories very well," confessed one
farmer, "but I felt Aberhart was a God-fearing man
who we could all trust. If he said Social Credit would
work, then I figured it would work."[6] Finally there
was Social Credit itself, the simple panacea that would
solve all the problems, the panacea that led some
people to line up at the city hall in Calgary the morning after the election to collect the $25 dividend they
had been promised.

There were critics of course. Social Credit had little
appeal to businessmen, professionals, newspaper
editors and the traditional middle-class leaders in
most communities. But these critics were already discredited because they had no answers and offered no
hope. They could only argue that Aberhart's nostrum
wouldn't work either, and in the mood of Alberta in
1935 the unbelievers received short shrift. Critics could
only speak bitterly of the disaster to come when Social
Credit was put to the test.

The test did not come quickly. Aberhart was in office but he had never promised to end the depression
overnight. In keeping with Major Douglas's theories,
Aberhart had always explained that experts would

[4]*Ibid.*, p. 238.
[5]*Ibid.*, p. 331.
[6]*Ibid.*, p. 262.

introduce the new monetary system and that the people of Alberta should judge, not the system, but the results. He had even warned that it would take eighteen months before there would be any results. In the meantime, the people must have faith in their leaders and be patient.

It is said that faith can move mountains but there is also the Biblical passage which says that faith without good works is dead. In his first eighteen months in office, Aberhart introduced little that could be linked to the idea of Social Credit. It was not that the new government did nothing; but what it actually did was really quite orthodox, or at least orthodox given the context of a prairie province during the depression. The legislation was a response to the problems of a debtor community, but it was not Social Credit.

Aberhart, for example, gave a high priority to balancing the provincial budget. He reduced expenditures and increased the sales tax and the income tax. This traditional approach to government finances was not unlike Aberhart's cautious and conservative management of his personal finances and the finances of the Prophetic Bible Institute. God-fearing men balanced their budgets and for all his talk of circulating credit and social dividends, Aberhart was still against deficits. But one of Aberhart's actions did shock conservative financiers. Alberta could not pay off a maturing bond issue in 1936; when the federal government refused to lend the money to the province without attaching some strings, the provincial government defaulted. Aberhart also unilaterally reduced the interest payments on all Alberta bonds by one-half for annual saving of $3 million. Responsible businessmen might be shocked at this repudiation of a solemn obligation but the aim—that of balancing the budget—was still orthodox, and reducing the interest rates on bonds was not illogical at a time when interest rates were low.

Aberhart also interfered with interest rates on mortgages. A Debt Adjustment Act cancelled all the interest on mortgages since 1932 and limited all interest rates on mortgages to 5 per cent. Again this was shocking, especially to eastern banks and mortgage companies, but it was a logical response to the plight of mortgaged farmers during a depression. Indeed, similar legislation was passed by other prairie governments and even the federal government had passed legislation for debt readjustment. Aberhart was more authoritarian in his approach—there were no consultations with the creditors and no arbitration proceedings—but otherwise his debt legislation did not differ from the policies of other governments in office. The *Financial Post*, not surprisingly, labelled this as communism but it could be better described as populism. It had no connection with the philosophy of Social Credit.

Aberhart continued to talk Social Credit and to make promising gestures in that direction, or menacing gestures depending on the point of view, but nothing really happened until 1937. Then the initiative came from so-called Social Credit insurgents, a group of some seventeen Social Credit backbenchers who had become impatient. These men insisted that Social Credit ideas be put into effect. The result was the Alberta Social Credit Act. This act provided for a group of experts to advise on legislation to introduce Social Credit. Two British experts, lieutenants of Douglas, were appointed and by August of 1937 their proposed legislation was prepared.

There could be no doubt that this legislation was pure Social Credit. One bill would establish local control over chartered banks in order to determine their

lending policies; banks which did not procure a provincial licence presumably would not be able to continue operations. The legislation was clearly unconsti-
tutional, dealing as it did with banking, a federal
responsibility. Indeed Aberhart's attorney-general
admitted this, and resigned for this reason. It is a
moot point whether Aberhart knew it was unconsti-
tutional, or whether he cared. In any case the legislation was passed. It was then promptly disallowed by
the federal government, using a power which had
rarely been used since the war. Federal intervention
added a new factor to the situation. To many Albertans it was yet another example of easterners thwart-
ing the people of western Canada, continuing the state
of bondage for the selfish benefit of bankers and the
"money power." At the next session of the Alberta
legislature, the same legislation was re-enacted, with
the wording slightly modified. There was also the Ac-
curate News and Information Act, which would compel
newspapers to publish government statements. The
justification for this was what Social Crediters saw as
"the organized press campaign of abuse and misre-
presentation" following the earlier Social Credit legislation.[7] Again this legislation was blocked by the
federal authorities; it was eventually declared *ultra
vires* by the courts.

The Canadian constitution thus prevented the Alberta government from putting Social Credit into practice. From a political point of view, this was not as
serious as it may have seemed. Aberhart could pose as
the champion of the people of Alberta, trying to keep
his solemn promises but being obstructed by eastern
financial interests. It was not his fault if he could not

[7] J. R. Mallory, *Social Credit and the Federal Power in Alberta* (Toronto, 1954), p. 78.

introduce Social Credit and end the depression. Eastern Canada was an easy scapegoat. This interpretation was further strengthened by yet another decision of the courts, this time on the Debt Adjustment Act, which declared that this act was also *ultra vires* because only the federal government could legislate on interest rates.

In retrospect, the startling and even shocking election of a Social Credit government in Alberta proved to be less significant than most observers had believed at the time. The theories of Social Credit were never implemented. Aberhart had been slow to act. It was not that he was insincere; it seems more probable that Social Credit for him was like the Kingdom of God. The millenium would come at the appointed time but in the meantime life must go on. And so like a sober Christian living in a world of sin, earning his daily bread and completing his three score years and ten, Aberhart had faced the immediate, material problems of balanced budgets and debt adjustment, leaving Social Credit for the morrow. Even when forced by his backbenchers to do something, the federal government intervened and Social Credit remained an ideal, a faith, an abstraction. In political terms, federal disallowance was an advantage. To Albertans the nefarious east had once more intervened to protect the vested interests to the detriment of the west. By the end of the decade the Social Credit government was firmly established as the champion of the citizens of Alberta against eastern domination. When war came, Aberhart and his followers proved to be as traditional in their loyalty to the crown as they had been in their attitude towards the budget. They accepted the commitment to king, flag and country without hesitation. By the spring of 1940 and the next provincial election, the popular support for the Social Credit party had declined but Aberhart was still returned with a solid majority. Social Credit had filled the political vacuum, the depression had strengthened the regional outlook of Alberta, Aberhart's image as an honest man of God had survived. The gospel of Social Credit was still expounded, but only as the theme for Sunday radio broadcasts and for election rhetoric. As with so many so-called revolutions, the astounding choice of the Alberta voters in 1935 had been less revolutionary than men had feared or hoped.

ATLANTIC BAPTIST COLLEGE
MONCTON, N. B.

10
Canada and the European Vortex

The decade of the 1930s began with Canadians, English and French alike, proud and boastful of their emergence as a nation, a North American nation. The bondage of colonialism was a thing of the past; the Statute of Westminster of 1931 was a formal recognition that Canada had achieved a new status and was in no way subordinate to Great Britain. As a new nation, Canada had already been accepted on the international scene; it had a seat in the Assembly of the League of Nations and had even served a term on the Council of the League. But now that this new status was widely recognized most Canadians were content to let matters rest. They had little interest in international affairs and certainly no desire to play a major role in international diplomacy. Europe seemed more and more remote. The Great War was still thought of as the war to end all wars. Once the war had been won, Canadians became absorbed in the prosperous spiral of the 1920s and then, less willingly, in the problems of the depression. European crises were like remote earthquakes or famines; they made the headlines but they were soon forgotten.

By the end of the decade, however, Canadian troops were once more in Europe and Canadians were again talking about a crusade to save democracy, to save British liberties and to save civilization. Britain and France had re-emerged as the ramparts of Canadian liberty, and Canadian security and Canada's future were identified with the fate of Europe. This transformation seems all the more remarkable when it is remembered that the rest of the North American continent still maintained its isolation. The United States did not go to war in 1939; nor did any other country in North or South America. Indeed, the Pan-American Union, with representatives from all American states except Canada, formally announced their unanimous intention not to become involved in the European conflict. In the new world only Canada declared war when Poland was invaded by Germany.

This poses some basic questions about the Canada of those years. What had happened to involve Canadians so closely in the affairs of a distant Europe, or, to put it differently, what brought Europe closer to Canada by 1939? What was there about Canada which distinguished it from other American nations, made it less isolated, less American, and more European than its new-world neighbours? Why did Canadians consider that their interests were so directly involved that they were prepared to return to the battlefields of Europe when other North Americans remained on the sidelines?

The depression does not provide the answer. If anything the depression had forced Canadians to turn inwards, to concentrate on Canadian problems and to try to raise themselves from the slough of economic stagnation by their own bootstraps. Unemployment and farm relief, fiscal and monetary policy, federal-provincial relations: these were domestic issues and the debates which revolved about them focused on the Canadian context. The one contrast with the United States was the importance to Canada of foreign markets. There could be no relief for Canadian farmers, Canadian loggers or Canadian miners if foreigners would not buy Canadian products. The United States could try to bring its production and consumption into balance and restore prosperity at home while the rest of the world lagged behind. Canadians could never forget that there could be no prosperity until other countries could buy Canadian exports. Even R.B. Bennett with his high tariff policy had tried to restore trade within the Commonwealth by the Ottawa Agreements of 1932. It was true that trade with the United States had become more important to Canada with the expansion of the pulp and paper and mining industries in the 1920s, and that a trade agreement with the United States was sought by both Bennett and Mackenzie King, but Great Britain was still Canada's major market for wheat and other farm products. Canada was less isolated from Europe than the United States because its trading links were more substantial.

This is not to suggest a kind of economic determinism, or to argue that Canada was necessarily involved in the European war to protect her economic interests. In 1939 the British navy still seemed to rule the waves and nobody believed that the Atlantic trade routes would be seriously disrupted. Trade meant closer contacts with Europe but if commerce had been the only link with Europe it is probable that Canada, like the

United States, would have been benevolently neutral, at least until the fall of France.

Nor is it possible to explain Canadian participation in 1939 in terms of a war against fascism. Many Canadians were repelled by Hitler's treatment of the Jews and by German aggression in Czechoslovakia and Poland. But nations rarely go to war for purely ideological reasons. Canadians who are repelled by apartheid in South Africa or by American intervention in Vietnam do not suggest that Canada should right these wrongs by declaring war. In spite of their repugnance for Nazi Germany, Canadians applauded Munich as bringing "peace in our time." Even six months later when Hitler occupied the rest of Czechoslovakia, Canadians expressed strong disapproval but never seriously considered going farther. There is nothing to suggest that Canadians were any more shocked by fascism than their neighbours to the south. And yet the United States didn't go to war in 1939 and Canada did. Canadian dislike for Hitler and nazism made it easier for Canadians to participate in the war, but it does not explain why they went to war.

This leaves us with one factor which does clearly distinguish Canada from other countries in the new world: the emotional ties to Great Britain. Canada, unlike the United States, had never fought a war of independence against Great Britain and for that reason Canadian patriotism had never had an anti-British component. Canadian autonomy had developed gradually without any major crises or bitter memories. Canadian identity was still somehow linked with the British connection, which served as a counterpoise to the influence of the United States. The link with the old world was still an integral part of Canadian identity and, when Great Britain went to war, loyal Canadians convinced themselves that it was their war too.

The ties with Great Britain were decisive. If Great Britain had not gone to war when Hitler invaded Poland, Canada would certainly not have done so. Canadians used many arguments to justify their decision: Hitler was a threat to world peace; the war was being fought to preserve liberty, justice, and democracy. But these were rationalizations; the majority of Canadians supported participation because they supported Great Britain. It was no accident that when Mackenzie King published his early wartime speeches he did not stress the horrors of fascism or the threat to Canadian survival. He entitled his book *Canada at Britain's Side.*

Canadian participation was not inevitable. The idea of Canadian troops fighting agåin in Europe would have seemed improbable or even unthinkable to most Canadians in the years before 1939. The long sequence of European crises—the Italian invasion of Ethiopia, German reoccupation of the Rhineland, the Spanish Civil War, the *Anschluss* with Austria, Munich, the occupation of Czechoslovakia, the invasion of Poland— these events all helped to prepare Canadians for a final European holocaust. Canadian intervention was also made possible, however, by the foreign policy of the Canadian government during these years. Gradually the unthinkable became the possible, and then almost the logical, decision for Canadians to make.

The growing concern for international affairs and the debate about Canadian foreign policy really begins in 1935 with the Italo-Ethiopian war. Japan had already invaded Manchuria but the Far East meant little to Canadians. Even Ethiopia was remote. But Italian aggression there affected British interests in Africa and it seemed possible that Britain would become involved. For some Canadians this would—and should—involve Canada too; for others it was a European squabble and no concern of theirs. Whatever the individual reaction might be, however, it was brought home to Canadians that a European war was a possibility, and that Canadians could not bury their heads in the sand forever. Would they, or would they not, participate if the time came?

In 1935 and 1936 the debate in Canada focused on the League of Nations, because Great Britain and France tried to restrain Italy through the machinery of the League. Most Canadians were ambivalent about the League. They had joined the League eagerly because membership was a recognition of international status, proof that Canada was no longer a colony. Membership certainly did not mean that Canadians had any great sense of mission as peacemakers, or even wanted to get embroiled in international disputes. It was a status symbol and not much more. In the early days of the League there had been some discussion of Article X, by which members undertook to defend the territory of other members against an aggressor. This was the key article for European states such as France because it was the guarantee of collective security. Collective security, however, was a commitment by member-states to go to war if there was aggression, and it was this commitment which had kept the United States out of the League. Canadians were opposed to Article X but they wanted the prestige of League membership. They sought a compromise by arguing that each member state should decide for itself what military obligations it would undertake. This meant that Canada could enjoy the status without necessarily taking any responsibility for collective security; it seemed to be the best of both worlds. As a Canadian delegate to the League once explained, Canada lived in a fireproof house and could not understand why Canadians should have to pay any insurance premiums.

This ambiguity only became disturbing with the Ethiopian crisis. Canada was represented on the League Committee of Eighteen which decided that Italy was the aggressor and recommended the imposition of economic sanctions. No League member was to export war materials to Italy. Bennett had instructed the Canadian delegation to support this position on the Committee, and when King came into office shortly after, his government imposed the sanctions. The Canadian delegate, W.A. Riddell, later proposed on his own that the Committee of Eighteen should add such items as oil to the prohibited list. The King government disapproved of this initiative but was ready to cooperate if the Committee and the League itself agreed to this extension. In effect, the issue never arose because the Committee could not agree. Britain and France preferred to try to appease Mussolini and the question of further economic sanctions was still being discussed at Geneva when the Italian armies completed the conquest of Ethiopia.

The debate in Canada, however, forced the government to clarify its position on the League. Economic sanctions, if they had been more effective, might have forced Mussolini to retaliate, with a European war as the result. If this happened, what would Canada do? Mackenzie King knew that many Canadians would favour participation: the "collectivists" who believed in collective security and the "imperialists" who believed in supporting Britain. But there were also many Canadians—the "neutralists" or North American isolationists—who would oppose participation. Many socialists and many French Canadians, for example, believed that Italy was only doing what other imperialist powers, such as Great Britain, had done in other parts of Africa. Britain could go to war to protect its imperial interests in Africa if it wanted but as one French Canadian bluntly put it, he wasn't interested in rescuing a tribe of negroes.

King saw the political danger. The Liberal party drew support from Canadians in all categories and a decision for or against participation would split the party. King knew what this meant; he had lived through the First World War when the party had been shattered by the conscription crisis. A discussion with Ernest Lapointe, his French-Canadian lieutenant, showed how real the danger was. This discussion took place shortly after the Liberal cabinet had decided to impose economic sanctions but had not decided what to do if Italy reacted violently and war broke out.

> If the Government was to decide for military sanctions he [Lapointe] would resign at once. He also said that if we did not, and the question came to be one which we had to decide, he believed that Illsley [sic] and one or two others would immediately resign. In other words, if the question of military sanctions comes we shall have the old war situation over again, with the party divided as it was at the time of conscription. My own feeling is that, if Canada carries out her part with respect to the economic sanctions, we should not be expected to go further.... Our own domestic situation must be considered first, and what will serve to keep Canada united. To be obliged to go into war would force an issue that might become a battle between imperialism and independence. At all costs, this must, if at all possible, be avoided.[1]

[1]W.L. Mackenzie King, Diary, October 29, 1935.

The question never arose in 1935 because the League did not propose military sanctions. But King had been alerted to the danger, and he took steps to eliminate any risks for the future. King had never been enthusiastic about the League of Nations in the past but he had shared the fuzzy sentimentality of many Canadians; the League seemed to be a "good thing," especially for Europeans, and Canadians should give it some encouragement. But there were really two concepts of the League. One pictured the League as an international forum for the discussion of international disputes, where nations would argue their case in public, with the League bringing the influence of world opinion to bear in order to arrive at a peaceful solution. The other concept was of the League as a military alliance against aggressors. After his experience during the Ethiopian crisis, King was not prepared to accept the second version. Collective security was a dangerous principle in his eyes because it might transform a remote incident into a war involving all League members. If Canadians disagreed over participation, as well they might, the result would be disastrous for the unity of the country—and of the Liberal party. King was still prepared to support the League as an instrument of mediation and conciliation but that was all. In 1936 he went to Geneva to make this clear; Canada, he stated, was not prepared to accept "automatic commitments to the application of force."

King's speech was well received by Canadians. They wanted to belong to the League as long as the League didn't involve any military obligations. After 1936 many Canadians still spoke hopefully of the power of reason or of common sense but they no longer talked naïvely about collective security. The League continued to go through the motions; the Assembly met annually at Geneva and the Canadian delegation attended. For all practical purposes, however, the League was no longer relevant to Canadian foreign policy.

With the League eliminated, what was Canada's foreign policy to be? The choice was narrowed to two possibilities. One was isolationism, refusing to accept any obligation or any responsibility in case of a European war. There was clearly a widespread sentiment in favour of neutrality under most circumstances. Mackenzie King himself gave vivid expression to this feeling in a speech on foreign policy in the House of Commons in 1939.

> The idea that every twenty years the country should automatically and as a matter of course take part in a war overseas for democracy or self-determination of other nations, that a country which has all it can do to run itself should feel called upon to save, periodically, a continent that cannot run itself, and to these ends risk the lives of its people, risk bankruptcy and political disunion, seems to many a nightmare and sheer madness.[2]

But, nightmare or not, did Canada have a choice? If the King of England declared war could the same sovereign, as King of Canada, be neutral? What did membership in the Commonwealth mean if one dominion could keep on the sidelines? Expressed in this way it was a legal or constitutional question, and much of the debate focused on constitutional precedents. But this was not the real question. If Canadians wanted to remain neutral a way could be found even if it meant ending the Commonwealth connection. But did Canadians want to remain neutral? Some of them did. The

[2]House of Commons *Debates,* March 20, 1939, p. 2043.

C.C.F. convention of 1938 formally adopted a resolution to the effect that Canada should "remain strictly neutral in case of imperialist wars" and the context made it clear that most wars were really fought for the defence of imperial interests.

On the other hand there were some Canadians who equated neutrality with disloyalty. The Conservative convention of 1938 opted for participation with Great Britain if war came. Arthur Meighen forthrightly declared:

> If there is one thing certain in this troubled world ... it is that the first line of defence for Canada—I go farther—the first line of defence for the whole of this North American continent is the British Empire itself. ... [Furthermore] No policy can be pursued in this Dominion that contemplates isolation and desertion, because such policy would split this Dominion in twain.[3]

The possibility of a split did exist. This explains why King favoured appeasement. If there was no war there would be no problem. It was hard to believe that any responsible leader of a civilized country would provoke a war; the memories of the carnage in France and Flanders were too fresh. Hitler denounced the Treaty of Versailles but many believed in retrospect that Versailles had been a harsh peace. Surely it was legitimate for Germany to reoccupy the Rhineland, its own territory, and even to unite with a willing Austria. The Sudeten question was more difficult. The Sudeten Germans were apparently unhappy under Czechoslovakian rule but the loss of the Sudetenland would make Czechoslovakia vulnerable to attack. But surely

[3]Senate *Debates,* January 19, 1937.

Hitler was a reasonable man, a sane man? If concessions were made he would surely be satisfied. Thus the policy of appeasement; the policy that was tried and is now looked on with horror or disgust because it failed. As late as Munich, however, most people believed, or hoped against hope, that Hitler could be appeased. The alternative was another war, an alternative too shocking to contemplate. Mackenzie King did not initiate the policy of appeasement but he encouraged it. At the time of Munich he was as relieved as was Chamberlain at the promise of "peace in our time." If there were no war there would be no split over the question of participation.

During all this time however, King followed what was described by his critics as a "back-seat" policy. From King's point of view the issues were European issues, affecting European countries much more directly than Canada, and the consequences of any decision would bear much more heavily on those countries than on Canada. It would have been possible for the Canadian government to express an opinion on many of these issues: it could have denounced German and Italian or Russian intervention in Spain, it could have criticized the *Anschluss*, it could have made proposals on the Sudeten question. It did not because King didn't believe that unsolicited advice from an outsider would do any good and it might make matters worse. As he said after the reoccupation of the Rhineland: "The attitude of the government is to do nothing itself and if possible to prevent anything occurring which will precipitate one additional factor into the all-important discussions which are now taking place."[4] It was not heroic; it was whistling in the dark. But as

[4]House of Commons *Debates,* March 23, 1936, p. 1333.

long as Canadians disagreed on what was required of them, they could only hope for the best.

Munich was the turning point. Until then King could believe that a war might be averted or, even if war came, that Great Britain might keep out of it. After Munich, he knew better. He could still hope, as one hopes for miracles, but he had to prepare for the worst.

King himself was clear enough about what his decision would be if there was a major European war in which Great Britain was involved. He believed that Canada should support Britain. He took it for granted that if Britain went to war it would be fighting on the side of right, the side of justice and liberty, and that it would only go to war if these values were threatened. Canadians were as much committed to these values as the British and should also play their part. What was more, King believed that most Canadians would want to participate when the time came. British institutions, the traditions and experiences of membership in Empire and Commonwealth and, for many, British ancestry—all these emotional ties would mean common cause with Britain in a crisis.

For King the question was not what the decision would be but how it would be possible to make the decision almost unanimous, how it could be made acceptable to Canadians who did not share those emotional ties to the same degree. As he saw it, the problem was one of preserving national unity when war came. King's solution to this problem was based on his analysis of the Canadian psyche. He used the analogy of the family. When children reach maturity they leave home. But for King this didn't mean that they cut themselves off from the family or took no responsibilities for other members of the family in time of trouble. The real danger to the family connection was that parents would impose too many restraints as their children grew up and that the children would react by rejecting parental authority, by leaving home and by cutting themselves off from the family. Applying this analogy to the Commonwealth King believed that the natural ties with Great Britain would survive if Canadians had the feeling that they were autonomous. With this feeling they would not have a psychological need to assert themselves—to prove that they were grown-up—by denying family ties.

On the basis of this analysis, King believed that Canadians must have the feeling that it was *their* decision to participate when war came. If there was the feeling that the mother country had made the decision for them, many Canadians would be resentful, would oppose the decision, and the nation would be divided. His strategy was to avoid any formal commitments to support Great Britain. In this way Canadians could be sure that their policy was not being determined in London. If war came Canadians would feel that they had a free choice: to support or not to support Great Britain. Only in this way, King believed, would the vast majority of Canadians approve of the decision to participate when war came.

The policy was baffling and frustrating for many Canadians at the time. Imperialists demanded an open commitment to be at Britain's side. King's refusal to make such a commitment seemed to many to be a betrayal of his imperial responsibilities. Isolationists demanded a guarantee that Canada would not participate in a European war. King's refusal to make such a guarantee seemed to many to prove that he was a tool of Downing Street. But King persisted. He increased the defence budget sharply in 1937 and again in 1939 but he denied that this involved any commitment. The expenditures on the army were not increased significantly because a larger army would imply an expeditionary force. Most of the additional funds went to the air force which could be justified in terms of coastal defence although, as King knew, a Canadian air force could play a role in Europe too if necessary. King also repeated time and time again that Parliament would decide; that if war broke out, Parliament would be called and would have to approve any decision to participate or not to participate. There would be no secret commitment, no clandestine agreement, no subversion of the right of the Canadian people through their Parliament to make the decision.

It was not a noble or a heroic policy. It means postponing the decision until the last minute. But King sincerely believed that any attempt to force an earlier decision would split the country. Many Canadians had first to be convinced that Canada could make a choice freely and autonomously before they could accept the idea of participation. Indecision was the price that had to be paid for national unity. After Munich King did try to prepare Canadians for the choice he believed they would make. As he said in the House of Commons in March of 1939:

> If there were a prospect of an aggressor launching an attack on Britain with bombers raining death on London, I have no doubt what the decision of the Canadian people will be. We would regard it as an act of aggression, menacing freedom in all parts of the British Commonwealth.[5]

He went on to say in the same speech that a war fought "over trade or prestige in some far corner of the world" would be a different matter, but it was clear that the

[5]House of Commons *Debates,* March 20, 1939, p. 2043.

Canadian government expected to be at Britain's side if Europe became a battlefield.

During the same debate Ernest Lapointe announced a major attempt to win support for a possible policy of participation. Lapointe spoke directly to his French-Canadian compatriots. He argued that neutrality would be impossible if Great Britain were at war. Formal neutrality would mean such steps as interning British ships in Canadian ports, for example, and most Canadians would never countenance such measures. He went on, however, to promise solemnly that if war came and Canada did participate that there would be no conscription. Participation yes, but conscription no.

Great Britain declared war on September 3, 1939. Canada remained formally uncommitted until Parliament was assembled. When the Canadian government introduced the resolution to declare war, there was almost no debate. J.S. Woodsworth of the C.C.F. and two French Canadians expressed their personal opposition but that was all. It was a striking proof of national unity. It was not national enthusiasm. Some were enthusiastic but for many the decision was accepted with reluctant acquiescence. But it was accepted; and so on September 10, 1939, Canada alone, of all the nations of North and South America, went to war.

In retrospect, it was the right decision. It seems obvious today that Canadian interests were at stake, that Hitler was a threat to the Canadian way of life just as surely as he was a threat to the countries of Europe. But the decision was not made on those grounds, at least not entirely. What distinguished Canada from the rest of the Americas were the links, however tenuous, with Britain and the Commonwealth. The formal ties were gone and the intangible ties were weakened by the 1930s, but they still held. Canadians, for all their talk of autonomy, had not cut themselves off from the old world.

11
Trends and Portents

The 1930s raised more questions than they answered. There was no political or economic revolution; governments were still operating on a small scale by contemporary standards and economic recovery was mainly the responsibility of private enterprise; most radical proposals had been watered down and any experiments had been tentative.

And yet it was a significant decade. The crucial fact was that new questions were being asked. Canadians had become aware of the modern problems of an industrial society and had searched for answers. Past experience was no guide and so, not surprisingly, the responses were hesitant and fumbling. People looked to

An earlier version of this chapter appeared in the *Canadian Forum*, April-May, 1970, pp. 18-20.

politicians for leadership and were often deceived. But
the importance of the 1930s is that Canadians for the
first time were focusing on the central issues of modern society. It was a necessary beginning, and many
of the structures and institutions of present-day Canada emerged from this beginning.

Politics was the obsession of the decade. Political
rallies drew unprecedented crowds, not merely because
they were the cheapest entertainment available but
also because only political issues seemed important.
The interest did not depend on the enthusiasm of the
orator or the originality of his message: even Mackenzie King attracted overflow audiences. Men who
had shown little interest in politics suddenly became
converts to political action. William Aberhart and T.C.
Douglas left the ministry, C.D. Howe gave up a career
as a successful construction engineer, Norman Rogers
left Queen's University for Ottawa. Everywhere discussions centred on political ideas. Literary criticism almost disappeared from the *Canadian Forum* and the
Queen's Quarterly because it no longer seemed relevant in a decade when catastrophe had struck. Politics was so pervasive that in Regina little-league soft-
ball teams were named after political parties, with
Liberals, Conservatives, C.C.F. and Social Crediters
battling for the championship.

For all the debate there was little discussion of the
decision-making process. Words like fascism, communism and democracy were part of everybody's vocabu-
lary but the focus was on results rather than on the
system. The Social Credit party in Alberta bluntly
stated that the voters should choose the experts and
give them all the power they needed. "The vast majority of people," said Aberhart, "are not interested in
details, and so are satisfied to express their will and let

somebody else do the job."[1] In Quebec, Abbé Groulx
went even farther. He longed for a *chef*, a leader who
embodied the virtues of the race, who could arouse
enthusiasm, demand obedience and impose the policies
which French Canada had always needed. "Happy are
the people who have found their dictator."[2] Few others
went that far, but academics like Harold Innis never
hid their conviction that economics was too esoteric for
ordinary men to understand. Even R.B. Bennett had
little confidence in public opinion and said so while he
was still in office.

> It is almost incomprehensible [he told a Con-
> servative gathering] that the vital issues of death
> to nations, peace or war, bankruptcy or solvency,
> should be determined by the counting of heads and
> knowing as we do that the majority...are un-
> trained and unskilled in dealing with the problems
> which they have to determine.[3]

So much for participatory democracy. Everybody could
agree that the economic system had broken down; men
were prepared to trust experts to bring order out of
chaos.

But who were the experts? What men had the answers to Canada's economic problems? Certainly not
the businessmen who in the heyday of the National
Policy had provided initiative and leadership. For half
a century the Canadian dream had been to create a
nation by exploiting the natural resources of the do-

---

[1] *Alberta Social Credit Chronicle,* March 22, 1935.
[2] L. Groulx (under the pseudonym of J. Brassier), "Pour qu'on
vive," *L'Action nationale,* janvier, 1934. (Translation)
[3] R. B. Bennett, "Democracy on Trial," *Canadian Problems*
(Toronto, 1934), p. 13.

minion as quickly as possible. There had been a sense of national purpose and of national urgency. The entrepreneurs and the captains of industry had been the great patriots, the makers of Canada, with fortunes and titles as their reward. Within a few years all this was changed. Somebody was to blame for the depression and businessmen were the obvious scapegoats. These former pillars of Canadian society were now seen as plutocrats, men who closed down factories and foreclosed mortgages, who worshipped profits with a callous disregard for the poverty and suffering they caused. Business ethics had not changed but public attitudes had. Profits were equated with profiteering and it became almost immoral to be rich. The new leaders of the 1930s would not be found in executive suites.

This meant a profound change in Canadian politics. The National Policy had been a joint enterprise based on the close cooperation between businessmen and politicians. The connection was so intimate that the distinction between public and private enterprise had been blurred. R.B. Bennett, the successful corporation lawyer and millionaire, had seemed an obvious choice for the leadership of the Conservative party in 1927. Three years later, when a recession threatened, many Canadians turned to him to save the country. By 1935, however, business leadership had been completely discredited. Bennett was out of office and soon out of politics and out of Canada.

A new breed of politicians emerged to fill the void, and the contrast was striking. H.H. Stevens, for example, had a deep-rooted antipathy to well-established businessmen. He won instant popularity in 1934 by denouncing J.S. Maclean of Canada Packers and C.L. Burton of Simpson's for exploiting the poor. And yet if Bennett had resigned the Conservative leadership in 1935 after his heart attack, H.H. Stevens might well have succeeded him. When Bennett did resign in 1938 he was followed by R.J. Manion, a country doctor with a fund of backroom jokes but a man who had no connections with business magnates. The change in political leadership was even more striking at the provincial level. Men like Mitch Hepburn, Maurice Duplessis, and William Aberhart were populists, colloquial and undignified, far more at ease at village picnics than at boardroom tables. Their popularity, at least in part, was because they were not established businessmen.

And yet, with all this political ferment, the new leaders did not create a brave new world. They donned the cloak of social reform but the new politics differed more in style than in substance. Many of the new men were little more than opportunists. They attacked the traditional leaders of Canadian society but had little to offer that was different. Some of them, like Hepburn and Duplessis, soon renewed the old alliance between politicians and private enterprise. Others quickly became immersed in the immediate financial and administrative problems of government and any long-range objectives were lost in the struggle to survive. Widespread discontent had lifted them quickly to the seats of the mighty but discontent provided no blueprint for reform.

One of the difficulties was that Canadians had given little thought to the problems which the depression aggravated. Nobody could have forecast the intensity of the economic disaster but some of the problems were not new. There had been unemployment and agricultural crises before the 1930s; only the magnitude was different. But the danger signals had been ignored. Although Canada had become an industrialized country, Canadians had never faced the implications for workers and farmers. They had been so mesmerized by economic expansion that they had paid little attention to the increasing economic insecurity which accompanied industrialization. Even Canadian intellectuals had accepted the National Policy as Canada's destiny. They had concentrated on such issues as imperialism and continentalism and had scarcely noticed the changes within Canadian society. There had been no tradition of muck-raking or left-wing criticism of free enterprise. What loyal Canadian would attack the builders of the nation? To carp or criticize would have been un-Canadian. Workers were expected to work and farmers were expected to wear their sheepskin coats, cheerfully playing their part in this great national undertaking.

There had been some exceptions. J.S. Woodsworth and Salem Bland had judged Canadian society in the light of Christian ideals and found it wanting. They had offered the social gospel as an alternative but had made few converts. Wheat farmers had turned to cooperative action, but even the Wheat Pools and the Progressive party were less radical than they appeared. By the end of the 1920s they had been absorbed within the system; the Wheat Pools were operating on the Grain Exchange and most of the Progressives had returned to the Liberal party.

The almost unquestioning acceptance of the National Policy in the past meant that when disaster struck there were no alternative policies waiting in the wings. Politics had been to a large extent a rivalry between the ins and outs, between the party in power and the party that wanted power. Parties had promised to be more efficient and more honest, but they had not offered a choice between political ideologies. When time-tested policies and traditional institutions were unable to resolve the crisis, the need for change seemed so urgent that any new and radical proposals seemed attractive. Suggestions which once would have been ridiculed or ignored were suddenly taken seriously.

There was more passion than logic in the discussion. Men debated the relative merits of public ownership of the means of production, of social credit and of the capitalist system with little awareness of what was possible. The demand for social reform was too sudden and too unexpected. Canadians were politically unsophisticated; they wanted reform but too often they were deceived by rhetoric. Action seemed more important than analysis; panaceas were more appealing than definitions. Politics was not seen as the art of the possible but as the means of salvation, and political debate resembled religious controversies, with the choice lying between the false prophets and the divinely inspired. To some degree politics became the opiate of the people. Few Canadians could distinguish between impassioned rhetoric and practicable policies, so that when the demagogue and the reformer competed for votes, all too often the demagogue won.

And yet, the 1930s did bring changes. People looked to governments and governments tried to respond. No final answers were found to end the economic stability of an industrial society; but governments did at least mobilize society to provide temporary relief, to keep people alive, and they did grapple with the more fundamental problems of economic recovery. In the process the role of government expanded beyond recognition and new institutions of government were created. The present-day assumption that governments are the major agencies for social action has its roots in the depression.

The greatest expansion of government activity has been in social welfare. Family allowances, old age pensions, unemployment insurance, medicare—these are all attempts to reduce economic insecurity in an industrial society. The depression made this insecurity painfully apparent and made clear the need for government welfare measures. Another major area of government activity has been the encouragement of economic activity and full employment. The days are gone when families were expected to survive sickness and unemployment on their own and when economic enterprise was expected to be private.

This continuing expansion of government activities has required new men. The transformation of the federal public service began in the 1930s. Able men who might have gone into business were attracted to Ottawa where they could exercise power and implement new social policies. Many of them who came during the depression stayed on to become the key administrators for the next two decades. The public service also experimented with new structures. New institutions were created to meet the expanding demands on government services: the Bank of Canada, the Wheat Board, the C.B.C., Trans-Canada Airlines. These institutions were not based on any conscious social philosophy; they were pragmatic responses to immediate needs, and they have survived because they worked. What were once considered daring and radical institutions have become accepted as normal and essential parts of the federal government.

The decade of the 1930s was thus an era of transition. The fascination with politics reflected the loss of faith in institutions and policies which had been unquestioned for half a century. It was a period of turbulence and confusion. Traditional values were challenged and new concepts of society were formulated. The process of industrialization had been going on for decades but in the 1930s the depression suddenly faced Canadians with this new reality. The tragedies of the depression and the failure of governments to solve the economic crisis are only part of the story. Despite the chaos and confusion it marks the beginning of our contemporary political system.

Bibliographical Essay

There is no standard survey of Canada in the 1930s which might serve as a suitable introduction to the period, although many books covering a longer period of time do provide a summary treatment of the 1930s. At the other extreme there are specialized studies which deal with one aspect of Canada during the depression. Any bibliography of the period must therefore be a patchwork rather than a comprehensive introduction to the period. F. R. Scott, *Canada Today* (Toronto, 1938) is the best survey written during the decade.

The emphasis on politics in the 1930s is reflected in the secondary sources. There is no study of the federal Liberal party although H. B. Neatby, *W. L. Mackenzie King, 1924-1932* (Toronto, 1963) touches on the early part of the decade. J. L. Granatstein, *The Politics of*

Survival (Toronto, 1967) has an introductory chapter on the Conservative party at the end of the decade; there is no adequate biography of R. B. Bennett. The C.C.F. has received more attention and Walter Young, *The Anatomy of a Party: The National C.C.F.* (Toronto, 1969) is very good. K. McNaught, *A Prophet in Politics* (Toronto, 1959) is the standard biography of J. S. Woodsworth, although it is better on Woodsworth's early years than for the 1930s. Grace MacInnis's biography of her father, *Woodsworth: A Man to Remember* (Toronto, 1953) presents a more personal portrait. J. R. H. Wilbur has two articles in the *Canadian Historical Review:* "H. H. Stevens and R. B. Bennett, 1930-1934" (March 1962), and "H. H. Stevens and the formation of the Reconstruction Party, 1934-35" (March 1964).

The regional discontent of the period underlies all the political ferment. Studies such as S. M. Lipset, *Agrarian Socialism* (Berkeley, 1950), Dorothy Steeves, *The Compassionate Rebel: E. E. Winch and His Times* (Vancouver, 1960) and L. Zakuta, *A Protest Movement Becalmed* (Toronto, 1964) illustrate the diversity within the C.C.F. party. The Social Credit party in Alberta seemed so exotic that a series of studies was sponsored to explain it. C. B. Macpherson, *Democracy in Alberta* (Toronto, 1953) sees the Social Credit movement as a quasi-party system which developed in response to the pressures of a mature capitalist system in a farming region. John Irving, *The Social Credit Movement in Alberta* (Toronto, 1959) concentrates on Aberhart and the mass response to his evangelism. The response of the Liberal party in British Columbia is described in Margaret Ormsby, "T. Dufferin Pattullo and the Little New Deal," *Canadian Historical Review* (December 1962). Mitchell Hepburn's erratic career in Ontario is colourfully sketched in Neil McKenty, *Mitch Hepburn*

(Toronto, 1967). *Politics of Discontent* (Toronto, 1967), edited by Ramsay Cook, includes articles on Aberhart and George McCullagh, as well as Margaret Ormsby's article on Pattullo and Wilbur's on the Reconstruction Party.

Much of the provincial political history is still unwritten. There is nothing on John Bracken, the only provincial premier to remain in office throughout the depression. In the Maritimes even a colourful figure like Angus L. Macdonald has been virtually ignored. Maurice Duplessis has attracted more attention, but studies such as R. Rumilly, *L'Histoire de la Province de Québec,* Vols. XXXII-XXXVII (Montreal, 1959-1968) and H. F. Quinn, *The Union Nationale* (Toronto, 1963) are partisan and superficial.

Even the economic studies of the depression in Canada are meagre. E. A. Safarian, *The Canadian Economy and the Great Depression* (Toronto, 1959, reprinted in paperback, 1970) provides data on public and private investment in the major sectors of the economy. I. Brecher, *Monetary and Fiscal Thought and Policy in Canada, 1919-1939* is disappointingly thin on both thought and policy. The most useful economic histories are still the *Report of the Royal Commission on Dominion-Provincial Relations,* Book I (Ottawa, 1940) and the studies prepared for this Commission, such as W. A. Mackintosh, "The Economic Background of Dominion-Provincial Relations," and S. A. Saunders, "The Economic History of the Maritime Provinces." Regional economic disparities have tended to focus attention on the federal-provincial relations; in addition to this royal commission, J. R. Mallory, *Social Credit and the Federal Power in Alberta* (Toronto, 1954) and V. C. Fowke, *The National Policy and the Wheat Economy* (Toronto, 1957) are primarily concerned with the impact of federal policies on the prairie economy.

International relations in the 1930s have been seen primarily as the relations with Great Britain. N. Mansergh, *Survey of British Commonwealth Affairs: Problems of External Policy, 1931-1939* (London, 1952) is an excellent study of the policies of the dominions. F. H. Soward *et al., Canada in World Affairs: The Pre-War Years* (Toronto, 1941) is still the best study of the public debate on Canadian external policy. James Eayrs, *In Defence of Canada,* Vol. II (Toronto, 1965) adds a good deal of information on the development of government policy; H. B. Neatby, "Mackenzie King and National Unity," in H. L. Dyck and H. S. Krosby, *Empire and Nations* (Toronto, 1969) presents King's policies more sympathetically.

French-Canadian society attracted the attention of American sociologists in the 1930s. H. Miner, *Saint-Denis, A French-Canadian Parish* (Chicago, 1939) pictures a traditional peasant society framed in a religious context, threatened after centuries of stability by the end of the frontier. E. C. Hughes, *French Canada in Transition* (Chicago, 1943) studies the impact of industrialization on this society. P. Garigue has subsequently challenged this view of French-Canadian society; the best introduction to the continuing debate is M. Rioux and Y. Martin, *French-Canadian Society,* Vol. I (Carleton Library, 1964). There has been no comparable discussion of English-Canadian societies, possibly because they were not exotic enough to attract the attention of American sociologists; H. F. Angus, ed., *Canada and Her Great Neighbor* (New Haven, 1938) does survey Canadian attitudes towards the United States during the decade.

No study of Canada in the 1930s would be complete without a reference to the writings of the period and to the reminiscences of contemporaries. The personal impact of poverty is described in letters by depression casualties to R. B. Bennett, edited by L. M. Grayson and Michael Bliss in *The Wretched of Canada* (Toronto, 1971). Victor Hoar, ed., *The Great Depression* (Toronto, 1969) includes recollections of the 1930s by F. R. Scott and Graham Spry. James Gray, *The Winter Years* (Toronto, 1966) is a brilliant evocation of life in Winnipeg during the depression; Jean-Paul Desbiens, *Sous le soleil de la pitié* (Ottawa, 1965) is the closest equivalent for French Canada. Jean Le Moyne, *Convergences* (Montreal, 1961) describes the pressures on a young French-Canadian intellectual; *Le Journal de Saint-Denys Garneau* (Montreal, 1954) is a more tortured and introspective record.

Canadian novels provide another approach to the decade. Irene Baird, *Waste Heritage* (Toronto, 1939) is a realistic novel of the homeless unemployed. Sinclair Ross, *As For Me and My House* (Toronto, 1941; reprinted in paperback, Toronto 1957) is a sensitive story of life in the prairie dustbowl. The novels of Morley Callaghan with a contemporary setting include *Such Is My Beloved* (1934), *They Shall Inherit the Earth* (1934) and *More Joy in Heaven* (1937). The best novel of the decade from French Canada is Ringuet (P. Panneton), *Trente Arpents* (Paris, 1938), which is also available in translation as *Thirty Acres*.

The scholarly works of the period are often the best source for the sense of Canadian identity in the 1930s. The League for Social Reconstruction, *Social Planning for Canada* (Toronto, 1935) presents the views and aspirations of left-wing intellectuals in Canada. Some of F. H. Underhill's articles from that decade are reprinted in *In Search of Canadian Liberalism* (Toronto, 1960); and Margaret Prang, "F.H.U. of the Canadian Forum," in Norman Penlington, ed., *On Canada: Essays in Honour of Frank H. Underhill* (Toronto, 1971) provides a brief introduction to his political views and his style. Less directly, English-Canadian historians reveal the intensified sense of Canadian identity; among the major works of the period are J. B. Brebner, *Explorers of North America* (1933), and *The Neutral Yankees of Nova Scotia* (1936), A. L. Burt, *The Old Province of Quebec* (1933), C. P. Stacey, *Canada and the British Army* (1936), G. F. G. Stanley, *The Birth of Western Canada* (1936), and D. G. Creighton, *Commercial Empire of the St. Lawrence* (1937). For French Canada, the last three volumes of T. Chapais, *Cours d'histoire du Canada* appeared in 1932-34. These lectures may be seen as the end of the "bonne ententiste" school with Lionel Groulx, *Notre Maître, Le Passé,* deuxième série (1936) showing the vitality of the nationalist school.

BAPTIST COLLEGE
MONCTON, N. B.

DATE DUE

ATLANTIC BAPTIST COLLEGE
MONCTON, N. B.